MW00475784

OPEN AND RELATIONAL THEOLOGY

AN INTRODUCTION TO LIFE-CHANGING IDEAS

THOMAS JAY OORD

SacraSage Press (SacraSagePress.com)

© 2021 SacraSage Press and Thomas Jay Oord

Interior Design: Nicole Sturk

Cover Design: ProDesigns

Print (Paperback): 978-1-948609-37-1

Electronic: 978-1-948609-38-8

Printed in the United States of America

Library of Congress Cataloguing-in-Publication Data

Open and Relational Theology: An Introduction to Life-Changing Ideas / Thomas Jay Oord

TABLE OF CONTENTS

Preface. ix

1. Why 1

2. Open 27

3. Relational 49

4. Amipotent. 67

5. Present 91

6. Loving 117

Appendix: Who is Open and Relational?. 147

About the Author. 151

Going Deeper 153

Acknowledgements. 163

Endnotes. 165

Index 171

PREFACE

People across the globe are discovering open and relational theology. The paths leading to this perspective are diverse, and its ideas help many make sense of God, their lives, and our beautiful but sometimes painful world. This book introduces those ideas.

Scholars have explored and promoted the ideas in open and relational theology for decades. Some write books so technical only experts understand them. Others write at a level understood only by graduate students or theology enthusiasts.

This book is different.

I write so that most adults can understand. My goal is to inform and stimulate creative thinking about what matters most.

Some ideas in this book will strike you as radical, unsettling, even mind-blowing. They'll expand your awareness and change your life. I recommend early morning or midnight walks to process them. You'll have a lot to think about!

When most people encounter this theology, they respond, *"Finally!* Something that makes sense!" These ideas align with our deepest intuitions and everyday experiences. They match scripture well, although we must abandon some interpretations people have offered. Other people take longer to "warm up" to these concepts, but they eventually see their winsomeness and wisdom.

New ideas upset the same ol' same ol'. Those who want the status quo find open and relational concepts threatening. I'm among many forced out of faith communities, leadership roles, or teaching positions for embracing these ideas.

A few even scream "heretics" at me and others who accept open and relational thinking. Most who play the heresy card don't know what it means or how heresy charges are rightly decided. I recommend focusing attention on what *actually* matters. We're better off to flee the dogma police than let traditional nonsense keep us from living and thinking well.

A warning: I sometimes write about horrific experiences like rape, death, and torture. I do so, because those are realities in the world. Many books that talk about God ignore the horrors and heartache of life, presenting life as serene and rosy, parroting pat answers too.

Ignoring life's pain comes at a cost: irrelevance. Theology worth embracing must account for beauty and evil, warm fuzzies and intense suffering. But addressing these horrors can trigger some readers. So, I offer this warning.

Introductory books can't cover every topic or go into depth. I encourage readers to explore other open and relational writings. At the conclusion of this book, I offer an abbreviated list of writings and authors published in the last thirty years. I call it "Going Deeper."

I also encourage you to explore the resources at The Center for Open and Relational Theology (c4ort dot com). Sign up for the monthly newsletter while you're on the website and consider adding your voice to the People section. Other fine organizations promote open and relational ideas too, and you'll find links to them on the Center site.

This book can't say everything. It lays out essential ideas in clear and provocative ways. Even the basics of open and relational theology breathe new life into our quest to understand God, make sense of existence, and live well together.

Get ready for an adventure!

1

WHY

MONICA

Monica wishes she could ignore Christmas.

To her, the holiday no longer signifies Jesus' birth or giving gifts. For Monica, Christmas means rape. *Hers*.

For months, the Allenton Baptist Youth Choir spent hour after hour practicing its Christmas Eve musical. The grey church basement echoed as they sang, and while this was not Westminster Cathedral, the acoustics suited them well.

The missing ingredient to the nearly all female choir was some voices to cover the lower registers. So Reverend Sanders convinced Devon and Jaker to join. Both had graduated and had to miss some practices because of work.

Monica felt a spark when Devon walked into the choir room the first time. He walked with confidence and his eyes were shiny and misty all at once. She *liked* him!

In subsequent rehearsals, she would smile shyly or stand near him at breaks. Devon didn't seem to notice... until the last rehearsal. Monica caught him glancing her way during *Silent Night.*

"You should come over," he said after rehearsal. "We need to celebrate."

"Celebrate what?" asked Monica, slightly tilting her head and grinning.

"You know... the season. And no school... whatever," said Devon.

Monica slipped out that evening and walked through Lion's Park to Devon's place. She arrived to find him with Jaker watching the Titans vs. Patriots on Sunday Night Football.

"The others are coming later," Devon said as he let her in. She joined them on the couch watching the Titans lose (again!) and drinking a few beers. After the game, Devon asked Monica if she'd like to go to his room to play *The Last of Us* on his PlayStation. After a while, Jaker joined them.

And that's when it happened. She thought they were just a little too handsy at first. She pushed the two away and struggled; they were stronger. Monica wishes she could forget the rest.

This Christmas, she wonders if God *really* cares. For her. If God loves us enough to send Jesus, why didn't He love her enough to stop her rape?

Monica no longer believes the words, "Emmanuel, God with us."

JIMMY

Campfires have a way of inspiring reflection.

Jimmy organized a "Guys' Weekend" last summer in the Sawtooth Mountains of Idaho. He invited gym buddies and friends from a Bible study, figuring they'd all get along.

"I've been thinking about hell," said Michael as the guys poked at the campfire the first night. "I don't think I believe in it anymore."

"Whatya mean?" someone asked.

"Well... it makes no sense," Michael responded. "Why would a loving God send someone to eternal punishment? In flames bigger than those," he said, gesturing toward the fire. "God's supposed to be loving and fair. The punishment doesn't fit the crime."

After a moment, Hector responded. "I learned about hell at Bishop Kelly High School." Realizing not everyone would understand, he explained: "I was brought up Catholic and went to Catholic schools. I guess I'll always be Catholic."

"Sister Gracie read Dante's *Inferno*," Hector continued. "She showed us paintings of people in fiery caves, twisting in agony. Damned if it didn't scare the hell out of me! Or *into* me!" Hector laughed at his play on words.

"I was raised Baptist," Michael replied. "We didn't have pictures, but preachers described hell: white-hot coals, torture chambers, and laughing demons. I had nightmares! As I got older, talk of hell seemed more like behavior control: 'Don't have sex before you're married, or you'll go to hell.' Of course, that didn't stop me and most guys. Or girls, for that matter!'"

Several smiled and nodded in agreement.

Others joined the conversation. Some said belief in hell was important for curbing crime and resisting temptation. Others said "hell as deterrent" didn't work; people still hurt each other. Besides, a *loving* God wouldn't damn anyone to *everlasting* pain.

Some said actions need consequences. That idea prompted a discussion of God's forgiveness, and someone asked about Hitler. Does a rotten guy like him get off Scot-free? A discussion of discipline ensued. And on it went.

After an hour, Jimmy asked a question. He didn't intend to end the conversation, but his question had that effect.

"Is there a way to believe God always forgives and doesn't send anyone to hell," he asked, "but also that destructive behavior has consequences?"

ROCHELLE

"I'll put that on the prayer chain."

Rochelle heard this phrase often. It's the response her mother gives to news about sickness, job loss, death, accidents, or anything needing prayer. The "prayer chain" rallies "prayer warriors" to "pray down the blessing."

When Rochelle was young, the prayer chain consisted of a written list of phone numbers. Today, mother has gone digital: text messages, Facebook groups, email threads, WhatsApp, and more.

Critics say prayer chains are just church-endorsed gossip, but Rochelle has been pondering bigger questions. She wonders what prayer says about who God is and how God acts.

On their drive home from her sophomore year at Missouri State University, she mustered the courage to start a conversation with her mom.

"I've been trying to make sense of prayer," Rochelle began, "the prayer that asks God to do something."

"What are you thinking?" her mother responded, turning down the Beach Boys.

"Well, God doesn't seem to answer many prayers," said Rochelle. "At least not in tangible ways."

"It happens more than you'd think, Honey," said her mother. "But God's ways are mysterious, and His timing is not ours. You never know how the Lord will answer prayer."

"I guess," said Rochelle, unconvinced. "But do prayers really change what God does? Think about it: wouldn't a loving God help even if we didn't ask? You'd help me if I *really* needed it, right?"

"Yes, I'd help," said her mother. "But it's nice to be asked!"

"I get that," Rochelle said. "Maybe I can explain what I'm thinking by asking some questions."

Rochelle's mother nodded.

"Do you think God knows everything that will ever happen?" asked Rochelle.

"Yes," her mother responded.

"Can God make a mistake about this knowledge?" asked Rochelle. "You know, like God knew you'd never get pregnant, but, Oops! Then you had me?"

Her mother laughed. "God doesn't make mistakes," she said. "If God knows something is true, it's a fact."

"That's the problem," said Rochelle, "if God already knows what will happen in the future and God can't make mistakes, whatever will be, *must* be. It's settled."

"I guess," her mother said.

"When we ask God to do something," said Rochelle, "don't we think the future might be different because we asked? But if God already knows what will happen and can't do other than what He already knows will occur, why pray?"

Her mother sat in silence, eyes fixed on the road as her mind churned through answers. She wanted to believe God knows now all that will happen in the future. And that God can't make mistakes. But she also believed prayer changes things.

"Maybe I can ask it this way," said Rochelle, to break the silence. "Does asking God to fix something change the future... if God already knows what happens in the future?"

KYLER

San Jose has its challenges and opportunities. As the largest city in California's Silicon Valley, its residents know the meaning of change. They also know better than most what it means for people with diverse cultures, economic statuses, IQs, skin colors, and religious beliefs to live together.

Kyler's parents moved to the city early in the dot-com boom. Kyler grew up believing in the power of technology, and he now works at a high-tech company. He married Gary ten years ago, and the two adopted baby girls.

Kyler's been wondering what to teach his daughters about God. His mother was Jewish and his father agnostic, and they taught him the difference between right and wrong. But no one in the family talked about God, at least not seriously. As a result, religious people make Kyler nervous. For his daughters' sake and his own curiosity, however, he's been talking with co-workers about their religious beliefs and commitments.

Steve, a co-worker, has responded to Kyler's inquiries. He's passionate about Christianity and often quotes the Bible and theologians. Steve's been explaining complicated sounding ideas like divine sovereignty, eschatology, and God's hiddenness. Kyler's still confused.

Kyler and Steve stopped for a drink at the Goosetown Lounge after work. Following a little political banter, Kyler said, "I've been thinking about your beliefs and discussing them with Gary. I don't understand the details, but I am trying to make sense of your views."

"Understandable," Steve responded.

"I want to grasp your most important beliefs," Kyler continued. "You know, the forest and not just the trees. And I've got a question."

"Lay it on me," Steve said, focusing his attention.

"In your version of Christianity — 'cuz I know there are many versions — does my life have meaning?"

"Of course!" said Steve, surprised. "The meaning of life is to obey God and enjoy Him forever. That's your purpose. That reminds me," he added, "I need to get you a copy of *The Purpose Driven Life*."

"Okay," said Kyler, "but I don't understand how this fits with God's sovereign plan."

"How so?" asked Steve.

"Well, if God predestines us before time begins, we aren't free. Our lives are predetermined, like the computers at Tech-Pro. Without true freedom, our choices don't matter. And if my choices don't matter, I don't see how my life matters. What I do makes no *ultimate* difference."

"But you *can* be free," said Steve, "when you do God's will. You're free when you do what God ordains."

"You said that earlier," said Kyler, "but it makes no sense to me. You sound like a politician saying the money is here and not here!"

Steve laughed awkwardly.

"Besides," Kyler continued, "I won't teach my daughters God controls them, *but* they're free. I can imagine one of them coming home at 3 a.m. and saying, 'Don't blame me. God predestined me to be late!'"

Steve laughed. "I get it," he said. "It's a mystery. God's ways are not our ways. Unless you're God, you won't understand it."

"Maybe not," said Kyler, "but I'm searching for beliefs that make sense. I can't believe our life has meaning if God predetermined everything."

Steve sat for a moment, thinking. A server brought another Guinness.

"If God pre-decides everything," Kyler concluded, "freedom isn't real."

CHAD AND JENNY

The Covid-19 pandemic crept across the globe in 2020, wreaking havoc. It killed millions, hospitalized tens of millions, and caused widespread suffering. Most viruses contribute to the health and functioning of life on planet earth, but some, like this one, mutate and cause destruction on a grand scale.

I met Chad on Zoom during the pandemic's early months. He was interested in the doctoral program I direct in open and relational theology. It didn't take long for me to realize he was intellectually capable, and I would enjoy working with him.

Most of our conversation focused on the virus and its impact on his life. Chad's wife, Jenny, had died a month earlier from Covid-induced complications. Both Chad and Jenny had been in the hospital with the virus – Chad recovered and walked out, while Jenny did not.

Due to the highly contagious nature of the virus, hospitals quarantined Covid patients, separating them for fear of spreading the virus among visitors, patients, nurses, and doctors. This meant Chad and Jenny were isolated, separated from each other during the last days of Jenny's life. Chad never got the chance to say goodbye to his best friend and lifelong partner. None of their family could visit or say goodbye either. Jenny died alone.

As we chatted, Chad was reeling. He wept as he talked about his frustrations trying to arrange a funeral during a pandemic. And about loneliness. Chad was hoping the doctoral program might give his life direction now that Jenny was gone. He needed something.

Chad asked the same question hundreds of millions of people across the world asked in 2020 and beyond: "Why didn't God stop Covid-19?"

One poll says two-thirds of American Christians believe the pandemic is God telling humanity to change. Does that make sense? Did God send or allow the coronavirus to teach us a lesson? Are Jenny and millions of dead people changing their ways? And is Chad better off lonely? And what about those still suffering the long-term effects of the virus, causing mental ailments, disabilities, and loss of quality of life?

Wouldn't a loving God prevent needless suffering and death?

A BETTER WAY

This book offers *actual* answers to these questions.

In the following chapters, I explain how open and relational ideas make sense of God's love in light of Monica's questions about rape, campfire questions about hell, Rochelle's questions about prayer, Kyler's questions about free will and meaning, the questions millions of people ask about God and Covid-19, and more.

Without believable answers to life's pressing questions, theology is of little use. God becomes like a pepper shaker: sometimes you sprinkle a bit, but the food tastes fine without it. Why believe in God if belief doesn't matter?

Fortunately, there is another—and a better—way to think.

SURVEY

Two sociologists asked Americans what they believe about God. These scientists interviewed thousands of subjects and consulted surveys from others to learn which theological beliefs are most common. The project results surprised many.

According to their findings, 95% of Americans believe in God. That's more than what many experts thought, but the sociologists define God broadly enough to allow for greater buy-in.[1] Americans have God on their minds.

Most interesting to me were the particular views Americans have about God — what God is like, whether God acts or relates, where God is, God's attitudes, and so on.[2] Survey results show most Americans believe God is 1) Authoritative, 2) Benevolent, 3) Distant, or 4) Critical.[3]

Let's look at each.

An Authoritative God

Almost a third of Americans see God as the cosmic authority. For ease of reference, let's call those who see God this way, "Authoritatives." In this perspective, God is a judge who engages the world and punishes when people do wrong. An authoritative God needs nothing from creatures because that deity is entirely independent.

Authoritatives are more likely than others to think God is a literal father, wrathful, and one who uses pain to discipline. Their rationale comes from Bible stories, the Qur'an, and popular views about punishing those who commit crimes.[4]

Those who see God like this feel compelled to keep rules and want others to do the same. They value allegiance to leadership, commitment to the tribe, and personal responsibility. Loyalty is a top priority for Authoritatives. They believe we can have absolute certainty about what God wants for us and others.[5]

To simplify, Authoritatives believe in a sovereign Judge who punishes the disobedient. In the words of an old song, "Trust and obey, 'cause there's no other way."

A Benevolent God

Most Americans, no matter what model of God they embrace, believe God is loving. Some who see God this way — let's call them "Nurturants," because "Benevolents" is awkward — understand divine love differently than others.[6]

Nurturants make up about a fourth of the American population. They see God's love as constantly forgiving and consoling. God has moral standards but doesn't retaliate against those who do not meet them. Instead, God warns us about the negative consequences that come from sin. The Nurturant perspective sees God as assisting, healing, inspiring, and showing compassion.

The way Authoritatives and Nurturants think about God corresponds with what each considers effective parenting. Nurturants prioritize empathy and care. They value acceptance, cooperation, and taking the perspectives of others. Nurturant parents value free expression from their children but think moral guidelines help kids discern which expressions are positive. Authoritatives think good parenting is strict, demanding, and includes swift punishment.

Nurturants see God as empathetic and forgiving. They embrace "care and share."

A Distant God

Researchers used "Distant" to describe the God in whom about a fourth of Americans believe. This God is not active in the world, nor does He judge the deeds of moral creatures. Believers in a distant God rarely speak of miracles and think biblical stories should never be taken literally. According to researchers, many who initially described themselves as agnostic actually believe in a God who is distant.[7]

Let's call people who believe God is distant and nonjudgmental the "Permissives." A Permissive perspective sees life as having few or no boundaries, standards, or restrictions. Some Permissives advocate extreme tolerance and verge toward anarchy. Others emphasize the liberty to do what an individual desires.

Permissive parents set few limits, not wanting to impose standards and expectations. They value autonomy in their children. Permissives seek to tear down oppressive religious and political systems but offer little or nothing to replace them.

Permissives say God exists, and just about anything goes.

A Critical God

The least common perspective of God among Americans (16%) says deity does not engage creation but keeps track of what we do. The Critical God will judge us after we die according to what we do here and now. Although responsible for moral standards and the regularities in the universe, this God doesn't intervene in earthly affairs.

As one disengaged, the Critical God is unaffected by what happens in our lives or the world. God has no emotions and can't feel pain or joy. We see the handiwork of this God in the design of a universe created long ago in some way we cannot describe.

Once we perish, the Critical God rewards the righteous and makes evildoers pay. This punishment might be eternal torment, purgatory, or annihilation. The reward for the righteous is eternal bliss on streets of gold or orgies with a thousand virgins. While the Critical God doesn't punish or reward now, this deity enforces the consequences later.[8]

The Critical God, like Santa Claus, is making a list and checking it twice to judge who's naughty or nice.

CERTAINTY

So... what is the correct view? Which model gets God *right*?

That's impossible to know with certainty. Scholars like myself analyze details in these and other models. We break them into sub-models and those into sub-sub-models. And then argue about minutiae.

I believe an open and relational view of God makes the most sense overall. But I'm not certain. I don't know God fully, so I can't be 100% sure. I look at reality through limited and sometimes distorted lenses, which means my vision is cloudy.

I just don't know for sure.

Open and relational thinkers can't *prove* their view is the right one. Theological statements like "God loves us" aren't mathematical equations like $2 + 2 = 4$. They're not verifiable statements like we say, "Jesse Owens won 4 gold medals in the 1936 Olympics."

No person — theist, atheist, or agnostic — has perfect vision of ultimate reality. We all wear distorted lenses.

Those who think they've figured out God are closed. Like a ship come to port, they've "arrived" at a secure harbor with nothing more to learn. The rest of us continue searching, sailing the waters of life. We're open.

Searching doesn't mean we're fumbling about with no sense of direction whatsoever. We can both search and be on a journey that makes sense, gives joy, and contributes to living well. We can find an escapade of significance between utter ignorance and absolute certainty.

To put it bluntly: some portrayals of God *are* better than others. Some are more plausible, for instance. Some portrayals account for the universe better. For our experiences better. Scriptures better or science better. Our intuitions or aesthetics better. And so on.

When it comes to God, we can't be certain. But we aren't clueless.

CONVENTIONAL THEOLOGY

On my way to explaining open and relational theology, it might help to identify theologies that are *unlike* it. You know, the alternatives. We can learn a lot about a view if we know what it opposes.

To avoid getting lost in the weeds, I'll use the label, "conventional God" for a host of views open and relational thinkers oppose. Under this label rests a potpourri of problematic ideas. I suspect you'll recognize many, others may surprise you.

Millions of people believe in the conventional God I describe below, and we could point to thousands of nuances within this perspective. Painting a general portrait is sufficient for the contrast I offer throughout this book.

Here are key features of the conventional God...

The conventional God exists above or outside time. Watching from this external perspective, He knows all that has ever happened and everything that will happen as if it already occurred. He's more like an abstract number than a loving sister; more like a definition than a person. The future is settled for this God in the same way the past is settled. And yes, the conventional God is usually thought of as masculine.

Call Him "the timeless God."

The conventional God is unaffected by what we do. Creation makes no difference to Him, because He can't be influenced. The conventional God never has a change of mind or alters course in response to creation, because creatures have no effect on Him. This God can't be compassionate in any sense that we understand compassion, because such love requires a response. Despite what people say, the unaffected God can't really respond to prayer.

Call Him "the uninfluenced God."

This God is in control. By either manipulating every creature in every instant or manipulating only those moments He deems important, the conventional God orchestrates history to a predetermined end. This means God either causes or permits all evil. The Nazi Holocaust? God did it or permitted it. Your cousin's car accident? God could have stopped it but chose not to. Child abuse? This God allows that too. The conventional God is large and in charge.

Call Him "the controlling God."

This God is pristine. He can't be in the presence of unholy creatures like you and me. We are dirty rotten scoundrels wallowing in the pit of sinful despair. To overcome this problem, the conventional God had to kill His Son. He now sees us through the lens of this atoning death and thinks we're pure when we aren't.

Call Him "the ultimate Germaphobe," and we're the germs.

The conventional God usually keeps a distance, preoccupied with His own glory. He's a lot like a narcissist. When necessary, He'll intervene to fiddle with creation or barge in where not welcome. The conventional God usually works through the laws of nature and natural systems He installed singlehandedly.

He occasionally breaks those laws and systems if it's important enough.

Call Him "the intervening God."

Our actions don't make a difference to the future the conventional God already knows as fact. He knows who ends up in heaven and who will fry in hell. We can't alter a future this God knows as settled and complete, because to alter it would make Him a liar. What we think are the beginning and end are a single moment to the conventional God.

Call Him "the foreknowing God."

The conventional God loves some people, sometimes. Maybe. Mostly He's mad, pissed at deplorable sinners who dare to disobey. This God usually punishes the unrepentant promptly, but on a good day, He may show a hand of mercy. Like the Roman emperor whose thumbs up or down depends on his own mood, you hope the conventional God is in a good mood. Don't count on forgiveness, because the conventional God can do whatever He damn well pleases. And "damning" is what He does well.

Call Him "the angry God."

I could identify more characteristics, but this should suffice. This vision of God sounds familiar to most people. It may sound familiar to you.

I don't believe in this God.

UNSATISFYING

Conventional theologies take various forms and have subtle nuances. I don't want to give the impression everyone who accepts the conventional model is unintelligent or naïve. Intellectually sophisticated versions of these ideas exist. But even the most sophisticated conventional descriptions do not convince me and others. Sometimes, the sophisticated versions are *especially* unsatisfying.

Did you notice some features of the conventional God contradict one another? God is said to be both angry at creatures and uninfluenced by them, for instance. If creatures can't influence God, how could they make Him angry? Or God is both timeless but also intervening. To intervene implies a time sequence in which God had not intervened and then did. Or God is both controlling but unable to be in our presence. How can an absent God control us?

Some conventional theologies correct these inconsistencies by choosing one feature and setting aside the other. This doesn't alleviate the problems, of course. Eliminating half a contradiction can make it more obvious just how bad the remaining problem is.

Other conventional theologies accept the inconsistencies and appeal to mystery, saying finite minds can't understand an infinite God. This kind of mystery helps no one. In fact, it adds another problem: unintelligibility. We end up with a schizophrenic God who is timeless but intervening, angry but uninfluenced, and controlling but not around.

Unintelligible!

Did you also notice the conventional view aligns most with the Authoritative and Critical models of God we looked at earlier? More than half of Americans embrace those views, and I suspect they dominate much of the world. The conventional view of God has deep, long-lasting, and worldwide influence.

It's time for something better.

NOT YOUR BOYFRIEND

Open and relational theology also comes in many forms. There's no one mold or type, no uniform vision everyone must embrace. Among the four models of God presented by sociologists, open and relational theology comes closest to the Benevolent/Nurturant view.[9] In fact, it's common for open and relational thinkers to start with "God is love" as they consider theology, their lives, and existence.

When asked, *most* people say God is loving. Eighty-five percent of Americans said so, according to the research. When many — especially theologians — explain what they mean by divine love, the God they describe sounds like a jerk! (Crass synonyms for "jerk" were in this book's earlier drafts.)

For instance, the God of conventional theologies has no emotions and feels nothing. He's apathetic, and that's just the start. The conventional God sends people to eternal torment, plays favorites, might choose to stop loving us, controls others, lashes out in vengeance, considers humans deplorable, and allows rape, genocide, and torture. (See why "jerk" isn't strong enough!)

The God of conventional theology is a Controlling Boyfriend in the Sky. Who'd want to spend eternity with Him?!

APPEALING REASONS

Open and relational theology understands God differently.

I'll explain the differences in coming chapters. Before we look at them, it helps to know *why* many people are attracted to open and relational thinking.

Below, in no particular order, are reasons many find open and relational theology appealing...

Answers Big Questions

A good number of open and relational thinkers arrived at these ideas after an intellectual quest. Some wrestled for years with questions about divine grace and sovereignty. Others wondered about God's relation to time and the future. Some looked for a solution to why a loving and powerful God doesn't prevent evil — "Why do bad things happen to good people?" Some wanted to harmonize science and religion. Others tried to reconcile their sense of free will with a powerful God active in their lives. Some looked for a theology that didn't imply God is an old white guy mansplaining morality. And many other questions that arise. Open and relational theology offers solutions to life's big questions.

Scripture

Open and relational thinkers believe sacred scriptures point to the primacy of divine love. Jews (and Christians) highlight the fifteen times the following words appear in the Hebrew Bible: "The Lord is compassionate and gracious, slow to act in anger, abounding in lovingkindness, and forgiving iniquity and transgression.[10]" Muslims build a case for open and relational theology from the Qur'an. "Allah is the ultimate source of instant beneficence and eternal mercy," the scriptures begin, "who encompasses the entire universe.[11]" Christians might emphasize "God is love"[12] and such other passages in the New Testament. God as described in most scripture makes sense in an open and relational framework.[13]

Logic of Love

Other advocates of open and relational theology start with the logic of love itself, irrespective of what any sacred book might say. They ask questions like: Does love cause or allow unnecessary pain? Does love predestine some to eternal hell? Does love control others? Does love concern itself only with self-interest? Does love make sense without freedom? To each of these questions open and relational thinkers answer, "No!" The logic of love leads to believing a loving God is open and relational.

Intuitions

Others come to open and relational theology by following their deepest intuitions. They may not have been exposed to any religion or have even rejected every religion, but they respond to truth, beauty, and goodness. A Source grounds and summons such responses. If this Source is loving, it must be relational rather than static, engaging an open future and not a settled one. The deep intuitions of many fit the open and relational vision.

Social Sciences

Another entryway to open and relational thinking starts by asking, "What if we took seriously research on relationships in psychology, sociology, communications, and medicine?" Then one asks, "What if we believed God relates in the ways this research says healthy people relate?" Studies suggest we're healthier when not manipulated, bullied, neglected, or abused. We are healthier when we're not doing the manipulating, etc. People who think God nurtures and who imitate that version of God have, on average, better relationships, greater psychological well-being, and more positive social connections. Some embrace what social science tells us about the good life and extrapolate what this means about God.

Relational Reality

Others have come to open and relational theology not so much to find answers but because it fits the way they naturally relate. This is a common entryway for some feminists, for instance. A relational God who engages noncoercively fits what many intuit is the best way to get along in the world. It fits existence top to bottom, simple to complex, individual to community. If we are open and relational beings in an open and relational world, why not think our Creator is open and relational?

Jesus

Many Christians point to Jesus as the primary reason they embrace open and relational theology. In their eyes, the persuasive love of Jesus — who re-presents God[14] — reveals God as one who loves nonviolently. Jesus engaged in giving and receiving love with others, believing their responses were not predetermined.

We best know what God's love is, say some, from the life, teachings, sufferings, death, and resurrection of Jesus.[15] Open and relational theology offers a framework to make sense of God in light of Jesus.

Science and Philosophy

Still others follow theories in science and philosophy to an open and relational view. Most physicists, biologists, and chemists find creation to be evolving and expanding. Some propose that a God who also evolves and expands must have created it. To make sense of morality and existence, many ethicists and metaphysicians propose the existence of an open and relational deity who grounds morals and calls existence toward complexity. A large percentage of scholars exploring issues in science and religion embrace an open and relational perspective.

The Perfect Being

One might come to believe God is open and relational through what some call "Perfect Being" theology. Instead of starting with scripture, science, religious experience, philosophies, or wisdom traditions, this approach asks, "What would a perfect being be like?" This perfect being is, of course, what many call God. If love is the greatest among divine perfections, one might deduce that a loving God is perfectly open and relational. Beginning with love overcomes contradictions in theologies that instead start with divine omnipotence, timelessness, or changeless perfection.

Artistic Sensibility

Artists and the artistically minded find open and relational theology attractive for how it fits their vision of the creative life. Imagining a new form of being or way of thinking fits nicely with a theology that says God acts in fresh ways and inspires novelty in creation. It would make sense that both the Supreme Artist and creaturely artists create in relation to objects and their own sparks of originality.

Meaning and Purpose

I conclude with a final reason some find open and relational theology appealing. The open and relational view provides a framework for thinking our lives have meaning and purpose. Most theologies portray God as one who pre-programs life or can get results singlehandedly. In those theologies, our choices can't ultimately matter. By contrast, open and relational thinking says we have genuinely free choices. Not even God can stop us. Because the future rests, in part, on what we decide, our lives have meaning and purpose.

These are some reasons a growing number of people find open and relational theology attractive. They build from diverse ways of living and thinking.

It's time to dump that Controlling Boyfriend in the Sky.

QUESTIONS:

1. Which questions in the five opening stories are most relevant to you? To which do you relate most?
2. What is the biggest question you have about who God is and how God acts?
3. Are you surprised by the research results describing models of God embraced by Americans? If so, what surprises you? If not, why not?
4. What aspects of the conventional God do you find puzzling, troubling, or unappealing? Give an example of a situation in which the conventional view of God influenced how people acted.
5. Which of the reasons many people find open and relational theology attractive do you find intriguing?

Scan the QR code for a video interview on God and the Covid-19 pandemic.

2

OPEN

Is God more like a caring mother or ruling king?

Think about it.

Notice I'm saying *more* like. Not *only* like. And not *exactly* like one or the other. If you had to choose, which is God more like?

And what about life?

Is life more like a vinyl record, each groove cut, and all songs prerecorded? Or an extemporaneous jazz session whose musicians improvise, exploring uncharted motifs?

Is life open ended or predetermined?

The way we answer these questions makes a world of difference!

THE FLOW OF TIME

To explain "open" well is to talk about the flow of time and the openness of the future. Open and relational theology says life is more like the jazz session. Nothing and no one — not even God — prerecords history. The future is open and yet to be determined. We're all in process.

Life isn't absolutely chaotic. It has patterns and regularities, habits and structures. Love, truth, and beauty are real goals with real influence. Existence isn't "anything goes."

Like an inspiring jazz band leader, a Guide nudges, gestures, and coaxes us toward creative expression. This Leader experiences the music as it happens, along with everyone else, uncertain where the tune will go.

It's experimental, not prearranged.

This leader of life—God—is more like a caring mother than a ruling king. God is more like a dance than a fortress, a chick-feeding penguin than a battling ram, an encouraging tutor than a bank security guard. If open and relational thinkers had to choose between God being more like wind or cement, wind wins out.

These "more like" statements point to a fluid, experiential, interactive, and nurturing God and universe.

The "open" in open and relational theology refers to the ongoing nature of time. Creation and Creator experience time moment by moment with no preordained future. In fact, there's no future at all... if we think "the future" is an already decided realm of completed events and settled facts.

The future doesn't (yet) exist!

POSSIBILITIES

Another way to explain "open" is to explore possibilities. Open and relational thinkers say the next moment is currently a realm of potentialities. What could be differs from what is. We imagine what *might, may,* or *could* occur. The not-yet-decided future is a field of options and alternatives available for selection.

If we examine our own experiences, we'll discover we already live as if the future is open. We live in the forward march of time and experience a relentless flow into the sea of possibilities. We think our decisions partly decide what will be, and already live as if these opportunities are a reality.

I'm not saying *everything* is up for grabs. It's not possible for Napoleon to rule France again. He's dead and gone. It's not possible for the United Kingdom never to exist. It does. I can't relive my high school basketball career; teenage Tom is no longer a possibility. The first punk band I joined will always be the first and never the second or third. That's settled.

The past is over and completed. It's done. The present is unfolding right now. It's happening. The future is yet to be decided. It's open.

God experiences the flow of time too. The past is past for God, and not even God can change it. The present is present, and the future is open. A Living Lover who creates, empowers, inspires, and helps also experiences reality moment by moment.

Creator and creation are in process.

A TIMELESS GOD

The open view stands in stark contrast to theologies that say God dwells outside time or watches the parade of life from a primeval perch. Those views assume God is timeless.

A timeless God has no experience of what it means to live moment by moment. A God who is in all respects timeless, in fact, can't do what we normally think a deity does. He can't respond to prayer, because "respond" implies a sequence of time. That God can't continue creating, forgive past sins, or expect love to win. A timeless God can't regret the Rwandan genocide, anticipate your next move in chess, or enjoy a joke's surprising twist.

A timeless God can't do anything new or continue doing anything He did previously.

Let me put a finer point on this. A God outside time can't know the past as past or the future as possible, because He has only a single present, an eternal "now." This deity can't experientially understand past-tense phrases like "she died," "World War II ended," or "the L.A. Lakers used to be located in Minnesota."

There is no past tense to a God outside time.

SCRIPTURE AND LOVE

God, as described in most Scripture, experiences time.

In the sacred texts of Christianity and Judaism, writers describe God *responding* to creation or *deciding* to do something new. These are time-oriented activities, not timeless ones. The Qur'an describes Allah as hearing, being patient, showing mercy, and living — all activities requiring a time sequence. Sacred scriptures portray the divine experiencing time.

Over forty times, biblical writers say God "repents." This doesn't mean God turns from sin; it means God has a change of mind. The Lover of Us All planned to do one thing but alters course to do something else in response to creation. A timeless God can't alter course, but a living God can. Scripture passages saying God chooses mercy, responds to needs, and liberates the oppressed make little sense if God is timeless.

And then there's love. It's hard to make sense of a timeless God giving and receiving in loving relationships. "Giving and receiving" assumes a sequence: first God gives and then receives. There's no relational sequence in a timeless God.

Almost every form of love involves emotion. But God as described by timeless theologies is emotionless in response to what we do. The conventional God may blissfully contemplate Himself but has no emotional response to creatures. Without emotion for others, the timeless God can't empathize with those who suffer or rejoice with those who celebrate.

In sum: conventional theologies portray God as timeless, so they can't portray God as a relational actor. These theologies don't fit the way God is portrayed in sacred scriptures. They don't fit our experiences as living beings. And they don't fit the reality and ways of love.

By contrast, an open and relational God experiences time's flow.

LIVE AND IN ACTION

Before the digital age, moviemakers shot movies on film. A filmstrip comprising single images moved rapidly through a projector's light beam. Although images were static, each passed across the light giving the impression of movement on screen. Early on, movie buffs called this phenomenon, "moving pictures."

Open and relational thinkers believe life and living creatures are a series of moments whose flow comprises existence. Time's flow is fundamental, and even the divine life advances moment by moment. Like images moving across a projector's beam, so the moments of God's life and ours create the story of reality.

The film and projector analogy breaks down in one way, however. The films we watch have been recorded, edited, and produced. A film director and producer pre-decided how the story would be told.

By contrast, open and relational thinkers believe each moment is created in *that* moment. The next frame is in the making right now,

and now,

and now,

and now...

A host of actors — from God to humans to other creatures to the smallest entities — write the story of life.

We're always "live and in action!"

FOREKNOWLEDGE

A God who faces an open future can't predestine everything. If God pre-decided it all, the future would be closed. This God ordained everything in advance, including torture, rape, disease, tragedy, accidents, violence, and ecological destruction. This God foreordained the Houston Astros to cheat in the World Series!

A God who faces an open future also can't be certain what we and creation will do. This God can't foreknow everything that will take place.

Open and relational thinkers reject the idea that God knows in advance everything that will ever happen. We think God has plans and purposes, and God knows what *might* happen. But God can't be certain about what free creatures will decide or what random events will occur until those decisions have been made or events happen. God doesn't have "definite exhaustive foreknowledge," to use a phrase common among scholars.

The argument against God foreknowing goes like this...

If God foreknows all that will occur and God can't make mistakes, nothing could happen other than what God foreknows. But to be free, creatures must choose among live options. They must have real say so or make genuine choices among possibilities. So, if God knows the future, creatures can't be free.

Let me put it another way. If God foreknows all with certainty, what we *think* is an open future must actually be closed. Instead of a realm of live options, the future must be complete, decided, and settled. Instead of being able to make free decisions about life and love, we're merely experiencing a simulation, like the Matrix. A settled future is inconsistent with our freely choosing.

If God foreknows all, freedom, love, and randomness are myths.

CHOCOLATE ICE CREAM

Let's look at an ice cream decision.

Suppose we're at a self-serve ice cream parlor on a warm summer day. We see Andee pick up her peppermint-striped bowl and walk toward the ice cream. She's about to select one of three flavors: chocolate, vanilla, or strawberry.

Suppose Andee's not sure which to choose. They're all delicious. Decisions, decisions, decisions! Her mouth waters.

Now suppose in some mysterious way it's already been settled, Andee gets chocolate. It's not a matter of whether she *may* get vanilla or strawberry. Andee *must* get chocolate. She's not free to choose otherwise, because it's been determined.

Notice the difference between *may* and *must* in this example. *May* assumes more than one live option; Andee may get any flavor. *Must* requires Andee to act one way. If she *must* get chocolate, she's not free to do otherwise.

The question arises: "Who or what decided that Andee's getting chocolate?"

People who think God predestines life will answer, "God settled it." Those who think existence is entirely determined by atoms, genes, or neurons say, "Nature settled it." Those who think we're determined by culture or upbringing point to environments and circumstances as determiners. People who think we're robots might blame our computer programs or programmer. One might even say, "It's blind fate."

Here's the key idea: saying God foreknows Andee gets chocolate doesn't mean God *causes* Andee to get chocolate. Knowing doesn't force anyone. Instead, God can only be certain about some future event if that future has already been settled, fixed, or complete. It doesn't matter *how* it was settled. Maybe it was the atoms, Andee's upbringing, evolution, or fate. Or some combination of these. What matters is that the matter was somehow settled before Andee walked to the ice cream. She's getting chocolate.

The point: God can only be certain about a future event if it has already been determined.[1]

Open and relational theists reject the idea God knows with certainty Andee chooses chocolate. God could only foreknow Andee gets chocolate if her doing so had already been determined. But open and relational thinkers believe Andee is free.

A settled future has no live options from which Andee can choose.

ALL-KNOWING

So... if the future is open and God can't be certain what will happen, is God ignorant? Does open and relational theology reject what scholars call "omniscience?" Is God not all-knowing?

No. God knows everything.

Open and relational thinkers say God knows all that *can* be known. God knows all that happened in the past, all that's happening in the present, and all possibilities for the future. God knows all mathematic and logical knowledge too. Knows what it means to be God. And so on.

God knows all.

No one — not even God — can know what's unknowable. If something isn't knowable, it can't be known. There is no *there* there.

LEARNING

But... and this might shock you... God can learn.

In each moment, additional information is generated in the universe (and in other universes, if they exist). God learns this new information as soon as it's knowable. God is like an all-absorbing sponge or all-encompassing database who inputs all information available.

Because God learns new information, God knows everything there is to know *and* adds new knowledge to the divine mind.

Let me illustrate. As I type this sentence, I'm deciding which keys to press and words to type. Before I started typing, God knew all the keys and words I might choose. But God wasn't sure which ones I would choose until I did the choosing. As I decide which keys to push and what words to add, God learns my decisions.

God's omniscience grows.

Add to my current decisions all the decisions made by deciders everywhere and all random events and all occurrences at the micro-levels of existence and everything else knowable... and you've got a mind-boggling amount of knowledge!

The One who knows all includes it all, moment by moment.

CHANGING?

Saying God adds knowledge leads to a question people have been asking for millennia: Does God change?

The God of open and relational theology experiences moment by moment in relation to creatures and creation. God responds, repents, redeems, renews, resists, rebuilds, receives, reconciles, regrets, rejoices, relents, remembers, restores, reunites, returns... and those are just the "re" activities. Each requires a time sequence. A change. A God who "re" acts *must* change — at least change in some ways.

But if God changes, is God reliable? Is this God trustworthy?

Could God love us today but hate us tomorrow? Promise peace, but bring calamity instead? Commit never to leave us nor forsake us but decide to leave us high and dry?

Is God your drunk uncle who can't be trusted?

To portray God as trustworthy, conventional theologies say God never changes. "Immutable" is the classic word. Read a few religious confessions and you'll find "immutability" championed. To many, a changing God is not worthy of worship, let alone someone to call divine. "There is no shadow of turning with Thee," as one hymn puts it.

Arguments supporting the "God never changes" idea appeal to a particular way of understanding perfection. A perfect God would not change, the argument goes, because change necessarily means lapse to imperfection. The perfect can only change to be imperfect.

Evangelical theologian Carl Henry put it this way: "God is perfect and, if perfect, can only change for the worse.[2]" Early church theologian Augustine spells out what he thinks this means: "There is no change in God, because there is nothing in him that can be changed or lost... he remains absolutely unchangeable.[3]"

PERFECT CHANGE

Some connect the logic of unchanging perfection to scripture. A few passages say God never changes. The most cited is Malachi 3:6, which says, "I am the Lord who does not change." The New Testament book of James repeats the idea.[4]

I've already noted that scripture portrays God doing activities requiring change. God gives and receives in relationship with creatures, for instance, and even repents. The Creator makes new covenants after old ones fail and making new covenants involves change. God is sometimes delighted and sometimes disappointed, activities which require a change in relation to what happens.

Scripture is full of passages that explicitly or implicitly say God changes.

Ironically, the verse just after Malachi 3:6 suggests God can change. "From the days of your fathers," the Lord continues, "you have turned away from my statutes and have not kept them. Return to me, and I will return to you.[5]"

To "return" is to change. It's a "re" word. The Lord promises to do a new activity — make a change — should the people return.

Conventional theologies focus on scripture passages that say God never changes but cannot account for those saying God changes. And those passages are common.

STABLE AND STEADFAST

How can God be unchanging in one verse but promise to change in the next?

The best answer emerged in the 20th century, and it came from the open and relational community.[6] This solution distinguishes God's essence from God's experience. God's essence is eternally unchanging; it's stable and steadfast. But God's experience changes moment by moment; it's flexible and forming. The divine experience is like the growing universe. It changes.

God is unchanging in one respect but changes in another.

To understand this, consider your life. You've been a human as long as you've been alive. That's stable. Your experience changes year by year, day by day, moment by moment. That's flexible. You're not the same human you were as a toddler. You're not even the same as you were yesterday, at least not *exactly* the same.

Your human essence never changes while your human experience always changes. *That* you're a human remains constant, *how* you live humanly changes moment by moment.[7]

God is a living, universally active but invisible being. God has an *everlastingly* unchanging essence and an *everlastingly* changing experience. The Living Lover of All is relationally flexible in experience and steadfastly stable in essence.

I LOVE MY DAUGHTERS

The ways of love illustrate how a person can change in one sense, but not in another.

My three daughters played soccer from age six until seventeen. I'd sometimes play this "beautiful game" with them in our backyard or neighborhood park. I love my girls and my playing alongside them improved their skills and knowledge of the sport.

When they were young, I'd kick the ball softly and use basic skills. I played gently and simply. As they grew older, my tactics changed. I kicked the ball harder, ran faster, and used technical moves to help them improve. And while I may not be Ronaldo, I have some "old man" tricks I used to challenge them. I did this because I love my daughters and wanted them to be the best they could.

Did my love change?

In one sense, it didn't. I loved to the utmost no matter their age or soccer skills. My love was unchanging, in the sense that I wanted what was best for them and acted to help improve their soccer skills.

In another sense, my love changed. I loved by changing the *ways* I played soccer. It was most loving to play gently and simply when they were young, but faster and more technically as they matured.

The fact *that* I love my daughters was immutable. *How* I expressed love mutated. My love was stable in one respect and flexible in another.

From everlasting to everlasting, God loves you, me, and all creation. That never changes, because love is an aspect of God's eternal essence. "The steadfast love of the Lord endures forever," is how the writer of Lamentations says it.[8]

But how God expresses love changes depending on what's best. God assesses how to help us and acts accordingly in each instance. Although the steadfast love of God never ceases, Lamentations also says it's "new every morning.[9]"

TRUST THE PROCESS

When I'm interacting with scholars, I use "essence-experience binate" to describe God's unchanging essence and changing experience. Others call it "dipolar theism." The name doesn't matter as much as saying, "God experiences time and changes, but God has a timeless essence that never changes."

Thinking God has an essence-experience binate helps us understand other aspects of the divine self. For instance, the fact *that* God knows all that's knowable (omniscience) never changes, but *what* God knows changes as God learns new information. The fact *that* God exists will never change, *how* God exists moment by moment changes. That God is compassionate remains steadfast, while the ways God shows compassion vary. And so on.

Those who say God never changes are half right — God's essence is unchanging. Scripture affirms this. Open and relational theology includes the other half of the truth. God's experience changes moment by moment in relationship with others, just as scripture tells us.

To adapt a phrase from the NBA's 76ers, we can "trust the (God in) process."

PRAYER MAKES A DIFFERENCE

To close my explanation of the word "open," let's look at petitionary prayer. It's common for people who believe in God to pray. They may ask God to act, teach, or help, hoping to get a positive response.

Suppose I want wisdom on how to handle a disagreement with my wife, for instance. Or maybe I want my daughter's kidney stones to pass as painlessly as possible. Or maybe I'm worried about the direction society is heading and want change. Or maybe someone's ill and I want to see them healed. Each concern might prompt me to ask for God's help, with the hope of a positive outcome.

At the same time, most of us have been praying long enough to know prayers aren't like coins inserted into a vending machine. Or like completing ATM transactions. We believe God hears our prayer and responds, because we believe a loving God would want to help. And while we don't control God, we hope that by asking, our request will affect the future positively.

Imagine what conventional theologies must say about petitionary prayer. Many claim God predestined all things from eternity. If all is pre-decided, my requests can't influence future outcomes. So, my prayers must be in vain. I can't get motivated to ask for help if the future has already been predetermined. What would be the point, right?

I also can't get motivated to pray for help if God already knows with certainty what the future will be. If God foreknows all future events, they must already be settled. There are no live options. What's the point of asking if the future is fixed?

I *can* get motivated to pray if the future is open and God is relational. What I say makes a difference to God and creation. The future is still in the making, and my efforts influence others and God. What I do matters.

I don't believe my prayers *force* God to do some task, of course. Nor does praying enable God to force some outcome by controlling people, other creatures, or circumstances. But my prayers become new data, pertinent information, relational input, and points of possibility that God can use in the next moments. My prayers are actions that generate new options. New avenues or opportunities might open to God and the world because I prayed.[10]

From an open and relational perspective, prayer affects the one praying, those being prayed for, and the God who responds.

An open future is different because we prayed.

UNANSWERED PRAYER

This view of prayer and an open future raises questions about *unanswered* prayers. Why do prayers sometimes bring positive results, but other times do not?

The answer depends in part on how we think about God's power. I'll address that subject soon, but to hint at my answer, I'll simply say God is always influenced and influential but never controlling. Chew on that for a bit, and we'll return to it soon.

I want to note something else as I conclude this section. People who ask God for help assume their prayers might influence God and the future. Things might turn out differently if they pray.

At least implicitly, most people already think and act as if the future is open and God experiences time. This includes most who intellectually believe in and teach a conventional God. They pray *as if* God is open and relational, which means their practice contradicts their theology. To be consistent, I recommend they stop believing in the conventional God and embrace the theology they already practice.

An open and relational God fits our assumptions about prayer.

INVIGORATED

I've been explaining why we should think the future is open for us and God. If we think everyone experiences time, we can make better sense of free actions, random events, and prayer. The open God changes in some ways but is unchanging in others. God learns and yet knows all that's knowable. I've said the God described in scriptures responds to creatures, which implies that God experiences time like we do.

Some open and relational thinkers find these explanations helpful, but they embrace open and relational theology more through intuition than these types of arguments or evidence. For them, saying God and creation move into an unsettled future fits their experience of how life works. They don't need syllogisms.

Whether one relies on scripture, arguments, or intuition, open and relational thought provides a sense of freedom.

Those who embrace it step outside confining categories, able to explore a way that reflects their experience of reality. Many feel invigorated. God seems more like a companion. Life seems expansive. Reality becomes a pulsing, living movement into possibilities.

Life is open!

I can't describe well how liberating this feels—deep in our psyche—when we realize the future is open for us and for God. It's like chains falling off the soul, light pouring in, and new horizons emerging that beckon exploration. It's a psychological, spiritual, and intellectual release words cannot capture fully.

Perhaps that's also why many find this view *so* appealing.

QUESTIONS:

1. What has been your belief about God's relation to time? Why has this been your view?

2. What's your reaction to hearing God knows everything knowable but there is no actual future to be known? How does this view differ from what you've heard?

3. What examples can you give (in scripture, common experience, and so on) of God learning? Or God having a change of mind?

4. How would you explain the idea, "God's nature never changes, but God's experience always changes?" How might this view comfort people?

5. How might you pray differently if the future is open and your prayers influence God?"

Scan the QR code for a conversation about freedom and possibilities.

3

RELATIONAL

Imagine an empty room large enough to seat five hundred people. Fifty people enter and space themselves at varying distances, in no particular order.

Bring to this room an enormous ball of string made of a single strand. Ask the fifty people to pass the ball among themselves in random order so everyone holds a point on the string. Eliminate slack. The result might look like a spider web or Native American dream catcher.

Now have one person in this interconnected web give a firm tug on the string. Ask others if they felt the tug. If the string is tight, dozens of people would feel at least something. If we added sensitive measuring devices, every point on this interconnected web would feel some movement.

Now imagine someone capable of touching this string at every point on the web. This person could touch 100,000 points, maybe millions. If she had a sensitive touch, she could feel every vibration.

Only someone able to touch all points simultaneously could feel the *full* influence of the one tug. Of course, touching all points at once would require the toucher to be in all places. The only one capable of this amazing feat would be omnipresent. And the One who feels every movement would be the most influenced.

An omnipresent, relational God is the most moved of all.

IMPASSIBLE

When I say, "God is relational," most people nod in agreement. God gives and receives in ongoing interaction, they say. The One who loves us best receives from us in mutual relationship. Like a marriage partner committed for better, for worse, for richer, for poorer, in sickness and in health... a loving God is relational.

"So, where's the controversy?" people wonder. "I thought open and relational theology offered radical ideas. Isn't this the God described in scripture and most spirituality? Doesn't everyone think God relates with us?"

"What may seem obvious," I respond, "is actually a minority view among leading theologians of yesteryear. And it's uncommon in some circles today."

Conventional theologies say we don't influence God. The deity they portray can't be affected by what we do, does not receive from creatures, and doesn't respond. Scholars say this God is "impassible."

As an example, take the most influential theologian in Roman Catholicism: Thomas Aquinas. "A relation of God to creatures is not a reality in God," he says matter-of-factly.[1] Influencing relations "are not really in Him" and "are ascribed to Him only in our understanding."[2] According to Aquinas, we may *think* God receives in relational response, but it's just our imagination.

Or take the Jewish theologian Maimonides. He connects the idea God never changes with the idea God does not relate. God "is mutable in no way whatever," says Maimonides. "There is no relation whatever existing between Him and any other being... and therefore no change as regards such relations can take place in Him." He contrasts creation with Creator: "despite the change and variation of earthly objects, no change takes place with respect to God's relation.[3]"

A deity who does not relate comes across as a stony statue or an unbreakable iceberg. There's no emotion and no empathy in Him. This God is the ultimate immovable object, able to resist any relational force.

An impassible God never relates.

RESPONDING

Most people intuit, if not consciously realize, problems with saying God does not relate. Open and relational scholars expose those problems using scripture, theology, philosophy, and more. It doesn't take an advanced degree to understand that a God who doesn't relate can't care about us or the world... at least care in any way we can imagine.

The conventional God doesn't play well with others. In fact, He doesn't play with others at all.

Consider the sacred texts again. Saying God is unrelated, unaffected, or uninfluenced stands at odds with Christian,

Hebrew, and Muslim scriptures. The overwhelming number of stories in these texts portray God as relating to creatures or creation. God is relational.

Consider our day-to-day relationship with God. It's impossible to have give-and-receive relations with an impassible and invulnerable deity. He can't respond to prayer, for instance, and isn't happy when we love or feel sad when we suffer. An impassible God could never console those who grieve. The unaffected God is an emotionless stick in the mud.

A non-relational deity can't do what a *loving* God does.

SUFFERING

I've written several books addressing God and suffering. In some, I explain that an open and relational God has compassion for the harmed and hurting. God cares on a visceral level. God feels.[4]

Readers often send me notes of gratitude. Many say they feel connected to a God who empathizes with their pain.

"I've had several miscarriages," one woman wrote, "and I felt so alone. 'Where is God?' I asked. 'Doesn't God care?' After reading your book *God Can't*, I felt such peace. A relational God knows and cares about me and my babies. God weeps."

"My prayers seemed to bounce like tennis balls off a brick wall," wrote one pastor. "Struggling with chronic pain made me bitter. I wondered why God created me and then made me endure such agony. It really wears on me! Your view that God didn't cause my pain but suffers with me really helps. I feel like praying again!"

One mother wrote, "Knowing God feels my pain helps when I feel the negative emotions caused by my son's bad choices. My husband helps me cope. So do friends. But they can't empathize like Abba God. A relational God really cares. Thanks for writing your book!"

I could share more notes. Each witness to the truth that hurting people need empathy. Without connection, they feel isolated and their pain unacknowledged. No human or pet connects with us perfectly, and none can feel *all* our pain. But a God who is always present, in all places, and in all aspects of our minds and bodies can and does empathize in ways that surpass any empathy we receive from others.

Conventional theologies say God can't empathize. It's not in Him. God knows about empathy intellectually, like a computer reacting to ones and zeroes. But not experientially. The conventional God can't be influenced, let alone feel anything creatures feel.

It's the nature of an open and relational God to relate with others. God suffers with those who suffer and rejoices with those who rejoice. We can imitate this God when we empathize with the downtrodden, broken, and bruised.

An open and relational God genuinely cares!

THE IMAGE OF GOD

"A God who suffers?" some respond. "Blasphemy! Heresy! Infidel!"

"Stop making God in your own image!"

Open and relational thinkers hear reactions like these from time to time. They come from skeptics trained in conventional theology or devotees afraid of change. No matter who raises the concerns, we should ask, "Do open and relational thinkers make God in their own image?"

The obvious place to begin answering is the first chapter of Genesis. "Let us make humans in our image," God says.[5] Many use the Latin phrase *imago dei* when pondering this passage, and it means "image of God."

No consensus exists about what it means to be made in God's image. At one extreme are those who think it means God is a bigger version of us. God is like King Kong, the Iron Giant, or a Marvel character.

In this view, God may have a bigger body, be smarter, much older, or stronger. Some biblical passages even support the "God's got a body like ours but bigger" view, but most reject it. Scholars call this "anthropomorphism," which means God has a form like ours.

Saying God is like us, but bigger or better, presents problems. If true, it means God has the flaws we have. A God like us might torture babies, for instance, forget your birthday, throw temper tantrums, break promises, decide to hibernate in November, cheat when playing cards, or stop existing.

Open and relational advocates don't think God is just like us. Although we're made in God's image, we differ from deity in crucial ways.

ENTIRELY UNLIKE US

At the other extreme are those who think God is *nothing* like us. We aren't like God in our actions, physicality, thoughts, relationships, or existence. Nada, zilch, zero. God is *not* like anything we say, think, experience, or imagine.

I call this view "absolute apophaticism," which means we cannot say or think anything true about God. It takes "God isn't like us" to an absolute extreme.

If God were totally unlike us, nothing we think about deity could be true. Saying "God loves" would be as true as "God xy&—xx>.nms(lqo*q." (Yeah, I let my fingers run wild on the keyboard.) If God is *nothing* like us, it would be equally wrong to say God is a Martian, Savior, mouse, metaphor, loving, idol, friend, phlegm, Yahweh, or stranger on a bus trying to make his way home.

If God is *entirely* dissimilar, we are not made in God's image. *Imago dei* would be meaningless fiction.

Open and relational thinkers propose ways to understand being made in the image of God that avoid "God is entirely different" and "God is pretty much like us."

THE BEST BOX

"Don't put God in a box!"

That's a line I sometimes hear when introducing open and relational ideas.

I might say, "God experiences time like we do." Or "God is relational like we are." Or something else.

In response, I hear, "Don't put God in a box!"

It takes only a minute of conversation to discover that the ones who criticize me put God in their own boxes. They might say, "God is outside time." "God doesn't depend on creation."

"God is sovereign." Those are just a different set of boxes people use to describe God.

If we want to say something meaningful about God, we can't avoid the "putting God in a box" enterprise. We all put God in a box. Even atheists believe something about the God they think doesn't exist.

I recommend we examine all the boxes in which people put God. Compare various descriptions, understandings, and revelations. Consider how each explains who God is and how God acts.

Then we should ask, "Which box is best?"

Open and relational thinkers believe a box that says God is open, relational, loving, emotional, omnipresent, influential, everlasting, and so on is a better box than the alternatives.

God is likely bigger and wilder than any box. But since we all put God in a box — in the sense of thinking God has particular attributes or acts in particular ways — I think we're wise to choose the best one.

GOD IS PERSONAL?

Saying "God is personal" carries negative baggage. To many, the phrase suggests God serves as a personal butler who caters to some at the expense of everyone else. A personal magician to fulfill our desires. "God's my G.P.S.," "God's my homeboy," or "God directed me around freeway traffic, and I saved 20 minutes!"

For others, saying "God is personal" suggests a divine body located some place. "Do you see God standing on the corner in that yellow dress?" we might ask. Or "my God can beat up yours, 'cuz He's got bigger muscles." Or "God sits on a mile-high throne wearing a white robe, white hair flowing in heavenly breezes."

Open and relational thinkers don't think God is personal in those ways.

Most believe God is a universal spirit without a localized body. God is "incorporeal," to use the classic word, which means "bodiless." Although incarnate in varying ways, we can't see God walking the dog or sight-seeing at the Eiffel Tower.

God *is* concerned about each creature, each entity, and the world. God shows concern without playing favorites. God also gives and receives in relationship like persons do. As one with intentions, plans, memories, and purposes, God is a personal agent. This meaning of "personal" makes sense.

Many open and relational thinkers use "relational" instead of "personal" to describe God. But both words are appropriate if defined carefully.

DIVINE EMOTIONS?

Saying "God experiences emotions" also carries baggage.

Theologians in the past distinguished God from deities in the Greek, Roman, and Egyptian pantheons. These deities experienced emotional outbursts leading to harm, manipulation, or deception. Creatures felt the brunt of these emotional power grabs. A deity whose anger causes suffering is not someone we can trust. Better to say God has no emotions, thought many, than wonder if God had emotions that would lead to harm. That God sometimes flies off the handle.

Others said God does not experience emotions because God is immaterial. Only physical beings feel emotion, the claim goes, so an immaterial God can't. The wind doesn't feel, so why think the Spirit does?

This "immaterial" claim has long puzzled me. How could anyone know an immaterial God feels no emotions? I think it's simply an assertion, and most people who make it are just extending their assumption that God isn't like us.

Some in the open and relational movement speculate God has a physical but universal dimension that's invisible. This would mean God isn't immaterial after all. Others claim God does not require a material dimension to feel emotions. If angels can be emotional (assuming they exist), why can't God?

The important point is this: open and relational thinkers believe God experiences emotions without thinking those emotions lead to moral meltdowns. God relates intimately with creation and feels all that's publicly feelable. But God's emotions never lead to evil.

Because the divine character never changes, God can be emotional without breaking bad and be personal without becoming your pool boy.

RECEIVING LOVE

In my twenties, I served as an associate pastor in Walla Walla, Washington (a town so good they named it twice). I preached occasionally, and the routine was for the day's preacher to greet people as they left the service.

As parishioners exited the sanctuary, many would express gratitude, "Thank you for that fine sermon, Pastor." Or "those were good words today." For some, I suspect these words were a mere formality. Others voiced them with sincerity, obviously moved by something I had said.

At first, I would respond to these gestures of appreciation with "Oh, it was nothing." Or "I tried!" Or "Well, I didn't say everything I thought was important." I thought humility required deflecting compliments.

Those who sincerely thanked me reacted to my deflections in ways that taught me I was not loving them well. Not accepting authentic appreciation robbed them of the opportunity to encourage me. Failure to receive their gifts of gratitude was failure to love in response.

So, I started saying, "thank you," to compliments. I was acting in love by receiving their love.

The idea that love can receive also plays out in my marriage. I love my spouse Cheryl by listening to her. My open ears and empathetic heart are a gift and became vital to deepening our relationship. I give the gift of listening to my children and to others. Receiving can be a form of love.

I must receive from others if I'm to love well. As I acknowledge their encouragement, I provide them an opportunity to love. And I receive information that helps me love well in response. I'm gathering data to love wisely.

When I'm ignorant of how to love effectively, even actions with good motives can miss the mark. Love might motivate me to give a box of chocolates only to discover the recipient is allergic to chocolate. Or pull an odd-looking weed only to discover it's a plant my wife just added to the garden.

Love as receiving—listening, learning, affirming, empathizing, and more—makes me more fruitful in the work of love. Without receiving first, I'm like a lawnmower salesman trying to sell machines to people living in desert sand.

This brings me to the relational love of God. As one who receives from creatures and creation, God gives the gifts of listening and empathizing too. Divine receiving validates creatures and their contributions. That's an act of love. But God also needs to receive creation's responses to love well in the next moment. God learns so that God can love effectively.

While God's nature is love, even God depends on relationships to love well in each moment.

THE PERFECT FRIEND

Imagine the perfect friend. She gets angry when the poor are mistreated and vulnerable oppressed. She's pissed! But she doesn't retaliate with revenge or repay evil with evil. She stands against injustice and acts to confront, comfort, and liberate. When you need help, she gives generously. That's a friend you can trust.

This perfect friend grieved when your child died. Or when your sister was raped. She mourned intensely. These genuine feelings don't sink her into immobilizing depression, however. She sits with you, empathizes, and makes tuna casseroles as she commiserates. She cares about you and those you care about. This friend is compassionate.

This perfect friend was the life of the party at your graduation. No one dances like she can! But she didn't trash the place or hog the attention. She has a way of lightening the mood, breaking the ice, and helping everyone have a good time. Your friend's a joy to be around.

This perfect friend helps without hurting others or herself. She acts for your good without becoming your "little buddy" who ignores herself and everyone else. You can't manipulate a perfect friend who works for the common good. Your friend has healthy relationships.

When you "just wanna hang out," this friend has time. Every day doesn't need to be a once-in-a-lifetime adventure, although a few days are. You don't always embark on the gargantuan task of "saving the world," but sometimes you try. You can count on this friend's presence for mundane moments too.

An open and relational God is like this perfect friend—but even better. You want a friend like that when you're battling at the gates of Mordor or relaxing with second breakfast at the Shire.

TRINITY

I conclude with an issue that divides open and relational thinkers. All say God relates with us and creation. That's the heart of "God is relational." But there are differing views in the open and relational community on God's relationality.

It's common for open and relational thinkers to say relationships are *essential* to God. An open and relational God is relational by nature, which means God *always* relates to others. God *is* relational in some essential way.

Among Christians, some say God always and essentially relates as Trinity. Three divine persons everlastingly relate with one another, so God is always and truly relational.

Scholars call this view "the social Trinity." Open and relational theologians like Jurgen Moltmann, Karen Baker-Fletcher, and Joseph Bracken embrace this approach.[6] In their view, God related internally as Trinity before creating the universe and thereafter relates with creatures. According to them, Jesus reveals such relations in how he talks about the Father and Spirit.

The triune God relates among divine members forever and with us today.

Because the social Trinity portrays God as essentially relational, it implies God is essentially timefull. Actual giving and receiving among persons assumes a sequence of moments: a gift is given in one moment and received in the next. Reciprocation follows. Even before creating the universe, says this view, God experienced ongoing time when relating internally among the divine persons.

Other open and relational theologians don't embrace the social Trinity. Jews, Muslims, and Unitarians in the open and relational movement reject it for reasons central to their faith traditions. They don't think God is three in one and have said so for millennia.

Some Christians also find the social Trinity problematic. They say this view amounts to believing in three Gods. That's tritheism. Keith Ward, Dale Tuggy, and Lewis Ford represent this group.[7] Most Christians want to believe in just one God—monotheism—so this criticism is significant.

Others say the social Trinity has little to no biblical support. Passages said to advocate the idea, they argue, are better interpreted in other ways. The Trinity isn't in scripture.

The key question is this, "How can God be one and three simultaneously?" One Church council or another has condemned every answer — including sophisticated ones — as heresy. I mean, "C'mon, Patrick!" (Google "St. Patrick's Bad Analogies.")

EVERLASTING RELATIONS

If an open and relational thinker rejects the idea God is a social Trinity, we might wonder how their God can be truly relational. A God isolated before creating would not *always* or necessarily relate with others. A God who once existed alone might be essentially timeless, in fact, only experiencing others timefully after creating.

Another group of open and relational thinkers believe God everlastingly relates to creatures and creation. No beginning and no end. God was never alone and timeless, because prior to creating and relating with our universe, God created and related with other universes. Therefore, God always and essentially relates with creaturely others without needing to be related in Trinity.

Saying God has always been creating and relating stands in opposition to the longstanding view that God created the universe from nothing. *Creatio ex nihilo* is the Latin phrase for this view. We'll explore it later, but I want to note that some open and relational thinkers reject creation from nothing and propose alternative creation theories.

A third approach unites the first two. It says God always relates in Trinity *and* always with creation. We might say God everlastingly relates internally among the divine members and externally relates with whatever universe exists.

There is no orthodox open and relational view on these matters. Some in the camp affirm the Trinity, others do not. Some seek novel ways to describe God as everlastingly open and relational with creation.

No matter their particular understanding of God as essentially related, all open and relational thinkers are committed to the idea God relates.

THE DIVINE EMBRACE

Open and relational theology embraces a relational God. And this God embraces us. This mutual embrace makes sense of how we understand love. It fits the way scripture describes God. It aligns with how the world works too.

Open and relational theology returns us to the ancient idea that a relational yet omnipresent person cares for everyone. It takes that idea and updates it for our day. In doing so, we see just how far conventional theologies have strayed from understanding God as lovingly influencing and being influenced by others.

The God of the universe is not unrelated and aloof. God relates with us moment by moment in giving and receiving love.

QUESTIONS

1. How might the idea that you influence and affect God change the way you live?
2. How do you feel about the idea God is a person?
3. What scriptural support is there for thinking God gives and receives as a relational actor?
4. The idea of the Trinity is difficult to fathom. Does it help you think about God as relational? Why or why not?
5. How does the idea God experiences emotions like compassion, anger, or sadness affect how you relate to God?

Scan the QR code for a video lecture on moment-by-moment choices in relations - Open Theism Conference.

4

AMIPOTENT

Imagine an extraterrestrial being sent you an email. And you responded. In ensuing exchanges, the alien asked you to describe human life.

What description would you give?

If I were responding, I'd begin by saying humans are diverse. It's difficult to know what we share in common. But if I reflected, I could construct a list of typical human characteristics. I'm not sure items on the list apply *only* to humans; other animals have some of these characteristics too. Nor am I sure they apply to *every* human; I haven't met them all. But I'd be confident that my list applies to most humans on planet earth.

I might begin my list with Rene Descartes' famous line, "I think, therefore, I am." Humans are thinking creatures, I'd say, although their thinking abilities vary. I'd say humans are valuing creatures. They make judgments about right and wrong, good and bad, beautiful and ugly — even though they disagree among themselves on these judgments. Humans assume cause and effect, and this plays a central role in their sciences, religions, family affairs, legal systems, and everyday life. I'd add that conscious humans have a sense of self, although they also experience themselves as relational, giving and receiving with others.

FREE WILL

And—coming to the subject I want to address—I'd tell my extraterrestrial friend humans are free. They have "free will," to use the common phrase.

I'd clarify: to be free is to choose, in a particular moment, among a number of options. Those choosing are a source or partial cause of the action they take. They could have chosen something else; they might have done otherwise.

Human freedom is limited, I'd say. It's constrained, conditioned, or framed by factors internal and external to the chooser. I call this "genuine but limited freedom." We make free choices moment by moment, but various factors and forces constrain us.

I'd admit to my alien friend that some humans claim free will is an illusion. But I'd report that everyone *acts* as if they make free choices, even those who say freedom is fake. Humans contradict themselves when claiming they're not free, but then freely choose. When their words don't match their actions, they're experiential hypocrites.

Freedom is an essential element on my "List of Human Characteristics."

SCIENCE REFUTES FREE WILL?

Open and relational thinkers affirm the truths of lived experience, and one such truth is that we make free decisions. They also incorporate the best of science when seeking to understand God, existence, and their own lives.

From time to time, someone in the public square will say, "science refutes free will." Although humans *think* they freely choose, according to this argument, they don't. And science says so.

Let's explore this.

In the distant past, deniers of freedom appealed to physics. The basic units of existence are entirely determined, they said, so humans made of those units are also determined. The atoms control us, says the argument, and we cannot do other than what they ordain.

The idea that physics undermines free will has today almost disappeared. Most physicists admit that at least indeterminism—chance and randomness—occurs at the smallest levels of reality. While indeterminism isn't full-blown freedom, it's not determinism either. Dominant theories of contemporary physics are at least compatible with human freedom.

Other deniers of freedom argue from biology. Richard Dawkins says humans are robots, blindly programmed by their selfish genes. The only evolutionary forces at play are random genetic mutation and natural selection, which eliminates free will.

But the idea that biology undermines freedom has also fallen on hard times. After all, biological organisms evolved from more basic units of existence, and physicists affirm at least indeterminacy among them. Contemporary biologists talk about self-determination, plasticity, dynamism, and probability in biology. All those words are compatible with free will.

Most recently, freedom deniers claim neuroscience disproves free will. A few studies claiming the brain acts before people choose seem to undermine free choice. If the brain acts before we consciously select among options, goes the argument, our neurons must control us.

Not so fast! Registering with our bodies decisions we made a split second earlier doesn't mean neural activity had no mental precedent. Minds can decide prior to or simultaneous with the actions our brains and bodies display. In short, neuroscience is compatible with genuine freedom.

Rather than proving free will is an illusion, the illusion is that science has no room for free will.[1]

AN EXPERIENTIAL NONNEGOTIABLE

There's an irony here. Scientists and philosophers who reject free will presuppose its truth in their actions.

Scientists choose some research agendas rather than others, for instance. Those seem to be free choices. For scientists to deny freedom after freely choosing a subject to research is an exercise in self-contradiction.

Philosophers freely choose to write papers. In some of those papers, philosophers deny free will. How odd! And why write papers denying freedom if you don't think readers can freely change their minds?

The actions of these people point to the reality of freedom.

Choosing is what I call an "experiential nonnegotiable." In our moment-by-moment experiences, we all make free choices. That's nonnegotiable. Even those who say they're not free act as if they are.

Science *can* help us understand freedom better. Research in physics, biology, neuroscience, psychology, anthropology, and more, gives us reasons to think free will is limited rather than unlimited. None of us is free to do anything we might imagine, despite what movie stars and professional athletes sometimes say.

Science also identifies *how* freedom increases. Humans are freer than cats, for instance, and cats are freer than worms. The more complex the creature, the greater the freedom. Social scientists point out that people whose basic needs are met enjoy greater freedom than those desperately needy. People with more education seem better equipped to choose among a greater range of options. And those relatively free from addictions enjoy greater freedom.

Science can be a friend of free will.

FREEDOM ARGUMENTS

Let me return to my extraterrestrial pen pal. To support my claim that humans act freely, I'd offer arguments and evidence. I might even bring in open and relational theology. I'd say we should believe we are free based on reasons like the following...

1. Belief in freedom fits the data we know best: our experience of freely choosing. We all presuppose in our actions that we make free choices, and we know this from a first-person perspective. Any robust explanation of life must incorporate our best-known data.

2. Belief in freedom helps us make sense of other creatures, especially humans. This fits nicely with what philosophers call "the analogy of other minds." I think of it when I consider how parents raise children. Nearly all parents believe kids act freely, and they reward or discipline accordingly.

3. Belief in freedom seems necessary to affirm moral responsibility. Without freedom, humans seem neither praiseworthy nor blameworthy. We might say moral responsibility requires free response-ability.

4. Freedom is a component of love. It's difficult to make sense of love if we're not free in any sense. Robots may do good things, but unless we define love oddly, we don't think robots love. Love requires genuine but limited freedom.

5. Belief in freedom seems necessary to affirm that we sometimes choose to learn. Insofar as students choose to be educated, this choice presupposes free will. Insofar as we seek to know, we act freely. Your choosing to read this book assumes freedom.

6. The reality of freedom accounts for freely rejecting the old and welcoming the new. Or rejecting the new and returning to the old. Conservatives appeal to freedom when wanting to return to past ideas; progressives appeal to freedom when calling us to embrace new ones.

7. People who believe themselves to be free are, according to scientific studies, more motivated to choose good over evil. Those who believe their negative urges are beyond control rarely resist those urges. And those who encounter evil are unlikely to resist it if they think nothing can be done.

8. We need to believe in free will to believe our lives matter. If God above or nature below predetermine all, our lives aren't ultimately significant. If all comes down to fate, we make no real contribution, because all has been determined.

9. Belief in freedom is most compatible with the belief God loves us. A loving God would give freedom to creatures rather than controlling them. This God would neither praise nor warn creatures if they were not free.

Open and relational thinkers believe humans are conscious organisms making choices about how to live, not machines remotely controlled by a Mad Scientist:

We express genuine but limited freedom.

OTHER FREE CREATURES?

What about other creatures? How far down creation's complexity chain does freedom go?

Some open and relational thinkers say only higher-order creatures like humans, chimps, dolphins, elephants, whales, horses, and dogs have free will. And a few old goats.

Others extend freedom to creatures apparently without self-consciousness like lizards, butterflies, and fish. Still others believe freedom or something like it is present even in bacteria, yeast, atoms, and quarks.

We find advantages in thinking all beings — from the simplest to the most complex — have freedom or something like it. Believing freedom extends to the basic entities of life means something or Someone did not interrupt evolution to insert freedom. Nor did free will emerge magically from non-free elements.

Saying freedom or something like it extends to the tiniest things allows open and relational thinkers to say God never controls cells, atoms, or even the simplest entities of existence. Creation includes free processes.[2] That helps when explaining evil, a subject I address later in this chapter.

The movie *Pocahontas* portrays how living nature acts. Grandmother Willow—a tree—advises Pocahontas, as other creatures and plants respond. J. R. R. Tolkien portrays plants as responding creatures in *The Lord of the Rings*. The Ents—tree-like beings that talk and move—shepherd the forest. The box-office hit, *Avatar*, extends the idea that all of creation is alive. These fictional stories point to nonfictional reality: creation is comprised from top to bottom with living organisms with agency.

The disadvantage of thinking freedom extends to the simplest beings is observational. I can't be certain other humans make free decisions, although what I observe them doing is like what I do when freely choosing. It's more difficult to be confident cells express freedom. We see responsiveness, self-organization, and agency among simpler creatures, but is this true freedom? Or environmentally determined reactions?

Open and relational theology doesn't rise or fall on the question of free will among quarks and amoebae. But it insists humans and other creatures act freely, although freedom is always limited. Most say free will is a gift from a gracious God who desires loving relationships.

God *wants* creation to act freely.

MOST POWERFUL?

Snow fell for two days. When Uncle Johnny, Aunt Kate, and 9-year-old Gracie left the reunion, at least a foot of fluff covered the gym parking lot. As they trudged to the car, relatives helped themselves to second helpings of Thanksgiving pie and watched the Dallas Cowboys on the big screen.

Johnny put the Camry in gear and pressed the pedal. It barely moved. The snow was too deep, the incline too steep, and worn tires had little traction.

Johnny stepped out to push and Kate slid into the driver's seat. He grunted and strained, calling out advice to Kate and swearing under his breath. Nothing. Little Gracie got out and pushed, but soon gave up. She walked back to the reunion.

"Can we get some help out here?" Gracie shouted as she stepped through the gym doors. Within seconds, a half-dozen people grabbed coats and headed outside. Joining Johnny, this quickly formed collective freed the car, and Kate drove onto a clear portion of pavement.

A few volunteers laughed at their rapid success. Johnny shook hands and slapped backs, as Kate took a big breath and exhaled her stress. The makeshift crew returned to the Cowboys, and the family of three drove toward home.

In this story, who was most powerful?

Uncle Johnny is probably 6′ 2″ and 230 pounds, but he couldn't move the car more than a few inches. Aunt Kate gunned the motor, but the wheels spun in place. The group was powerful, and their efforts proved effective.

But I think Gracie was the most powerful.

She asked for help. Her request persuaded powerful bodies to exert the combined effort needed to put the car on solid ground. Her call made the difference. In fact, Gracie lagged on the walk back to the car, and the crew didn't need her muscles. Because Gracie persuaded others to use their power, she was the most powerful of all.

That's what God's power is like.

LOVIFIED

As I've explained open and relational theology, I've added statements here and there about God's love. That's natural for an open and relational thinker. While "love" doesn't sit alongside "open" and "relational" in this theology's title, open and relational thinkers emphasize it. And most conceive of God's power in the light of love.

An open and relational God exerts open and relational power. God doesn't predetermine or singlehandedly decide all that happens but works with others in the ongoing adventure of life. As an actor, God convinces other actors who have power to co-labor.

Open and relational thinkers might say God persuades instead of coerces. Or that God empowers but doesn't overpower. Or that God invites rather than forces. They use relational verbs to talk about what God does: call, inspire, lure, insist, weep, trust, transform, give, risk, share, console, and more. They rarely if ever say God controls or abandons, because love wouldn't act that way.

Because God woos creaturely actors to cooperate with the work of love, divine power is "lovified."

CONVENTIONAL DIVINE POWER

Open and relational views of divine power differ drastically from conventional ones.

One conventional theology says God controls everyone and everything. The sovereign One has a monopoly on power. We often associate this view with John Calvin, but many others have said the same. From this perspective, an omnipotent God predestines all things, including murder, rape, and holocausts. This God is a puppet master: strings we can't see maneuver us all.

Other conventional theologies reject complete control but say God *sometimes* decides outcomes singlehandedly. This God is still in control, according to those who hold this view. God *can* dominate but doesn't very often. God only intervenes to ensure an important outcome or fix a broken wheel. He's like a babysitter who protects the children sometimes, but other times lets the neighbor beat them bloody. Those who embrace this view invent elaborate explanations for why a God capable of control doesn't stop *all* genuine evil.

In reaction to the first and second theologies, an alternative view emerged. It says God exerts no power at all. God voluntarily chooses to be uninvolved, taking a "hands off" approach to life. Scholars call this "deism," and it's the "Distant God" model we explored earlier. Good luck enjoying a loving relationship with the deity who, as Bette Midler puts it, is "watching us from a distance." Relational love isn't a reality with Him.

A fourth theology says God's actions are radically unknowable. They're literally inconceivable, like a mysterious black box no one can unlock. Any claim about what God did, does, or could do is meaningless, because this view says God is utterly incomprehensible. Might as well shut off your brain when it comes to understanding this God, because your brain can't help.

LOGIC OF LOVE

Open and relational theology offers a better way to think about God. It says we best understand God's power in ways consistent with our experiences and the world. It draws from scriptural stories and passages that speak of God acting without controlling others.

Open and relational theology uses the logic of love to make sense of what God can and can't do. If we think love does not manipulate, for instance, we should remove "manipulation" from activities God does. If our experience of freedom suggests God must not control, we remove "overrides freedom" from divine activities. If we think a loving God who *could* prevent evil *would*, we remove "God prevents evil singlehandedly" from activities God does. If we think love doesn't abuse, torture, or sell children into slavery, we take those activities off the list of things God does or wants from others. And so on.

Open and relational scholars use sophisticated arguments to explain their views. They draw from scriptures, philosophy, experience, and more. Most of this work occurs at academic conferences, in scholarly books, or websites dedicated to complex ideas. To explore them, check out those resources at the conclusion of this book.

An open, relational, and loving God acts, but does not control.

THE POWER PROPOSALS

"But *why* is God's power relational and persuasive?" we might ask.

Some open and relational theologians think that after creating the universe, God chose to self-limit. Out of love, says this view, God gives freedom and agency to creatures, metaphorically withdrawing to allow them autonomous choice. I call this "voluntary divine self-limitation."

Others think metaphysical laws or the God-world relationship prevent God from controlling. In this view, God isn't choosing to be persuasive; persuasion is built into the structures of existence. God can't unilaterally determine others, because it's impossible.

Still others appeal to the logic of free will. For them, God can't simultaneously grant freedom and not grant it. That's not logical. Giving free will means God can't control those to whom the gift is given. These free agents might include people, animals, birds, angels, demons, or more. A God who gives freedom can't control what happens.

My view says God can't control, because uncontrolling love comes first in God's unchanging nature. Because God can't deny the divine nature, God can't control anyone or anything.

As I see it, outside forces or factors don't constrain God. Nor does God voluntarily self-limit. God necessarily expresses self-giving and others-empowering love, because that's what divine love does. I call this "the uncontrolling love of God" or the "essential kenosis" view.[3]

None of the views I've listed say God is absent from our lives or the world. Open and relational thinkers don't believe God sits on Mars eating popcorn, uninvolved in the affairs of planet earth. God isn't sitting in the upper deck watching the ballgame below.

These views also reject a "do-nothing" God. God isn't a couch potato who eats your ice cream but never helps to clean the house. The Creator and Sustainer is more than the glue of the universe, more than a noninteractive Ground of Being. God is active rather than inert.

God is a universal agent who acts directly in relation to creation, without controlling.

Notice also that open and relational thinkers offer proposals about how God really acts. They aren't saying, "God's ways aren't anything like ours." Instead of a mysterious black box, they propose understandable models to describe divine activity. They use analogies connected to creaturely action. To put it in language we explored earlier, open and relational thinkers put God in a box like everyone else, they just think their box is better than the alternative.

AMIPOTENT

The open and relational God is not impotent. This God is no wimp or wussy, in the sense of being weak or doing nothing. No one is more powerful. An open and relational God influences all creation, all the time, forever.

But this God isn't omnipotent either. At least not omnipotent in the conventional sense of doing everything or being in control. Omnipotence as popularly understood makes no sense in light of scriptures and the way we experience life.

Besides, when careful thinkers qualify omnipotence — saying God can't do what's illogical, can't act in ways that oppose God's nature, can't override free will, can't change the past, doesn't have all power, and so on — the term's meaning evaporates like a puddle in the desert sun.

God is neither impotent nor omnipotent but what I call "amipotent."

I coined this word by combining the Latin word for power — "potent" — with a Latin prefix for love — "ami." From "potent" we get words like "potential" and "potency." We find the "ami" prefix in love words like "amity," "amigo," and "amicable."

God's power is the power of love: amipotence.

An amipotent God is active, but not a dictator. Amipotence is receptive but not overwhelmed. It engages without domineering, is generous but not pushy, and invites without monopolizing. Amipotence is divine strength working positively at all times and places.

The power of an amipotent God is the power of love.

GOOD PARENTING

While no analogy is perfect, comparing God's love to parenting can help.

Good parents nurture, care, instruct, and encourage. They exert the right amount of influence while empowering children to make their own decisions and become their own persons. Good parents instruct, but also learn from the children they lead. They foster positive reciprocal relationships. They parent forward.

Unhelpful parents try to manipulate. They hover over kids like a helicopter, trying to make or force each decision. "You'll like this food," they say, "you'll play that sport," "you'll learn this musical instrument," or "you'll date this person." The implicit message is simple: "Obey, as I rule. Pretend to choose freely while I actually call the shots."

Other unhelpful parents withdraw and shirk responsibility. These misguided folks either leave their kids or choose an uninvolved approach to parenting. Because they offer no guidance or support, children experience them as cold or absent, standoffish, or unresponsive. Absentee adults fail to love their kids.

Like a good parent, a loving God neither manipulates nor abandons. The divine Parent loves through guidance, influence, and wisdom. God sees the intrinsic value of children and coaxes them toward a better future individually, corporately, and as a civilization. And we make a real contribution, partnering with the divine.[4]

A loving God nurtures.

Jesus called this loving one "Abba", which means "Daddy." He also said God is like a hen protecting her chicks or a joyous parent welcoming home runaways, throwing parties and giving gifts. A nurturing God adopts orphans and gives them a loving home.

THE ANALOGY'S LIMITS

The parent-God analogy breaks down, of course. All creature-Creator analogies do in some way. While embracing its assets, let's look at the analogy's limits.

First, even the best humans sometimes fail to love. Creatures don't have an eternal nature that includes perfect love like God does. The perfect human parent doesn't exist, because no human is perfect. By contrast, the God whose nature is love — "God is love" — exists and always loves perfectly.

Second, human parents can't *always* influence their children, because they aren't omnipresent. Humans act in one place at one time, but their children may be off at school, at daycare, over at friends, or studying at university. A universal God is always present 24 hours a day, 7 days a week, 365 days a year. And February 29, when it rolls around.

The always loving and always present God always loves everyone and everything.

Third, God doesn't have a localized body like we do. Humans sometimes use their bodies to rescue children from harm or shield the vulnerable from attackers. God doesn't have such a body. Open and relational theologians say God inspires humans to use their own bodies to show love. When they cooperate with divine inspiration, they become God's metaphorical hands and feet. But unlike humans, the omnipresent Spirit doesn't have a localized body.

This last difference is important. It plays a role in helping us answer the #1 question asked by those who ponder God's power: the problem of evil.

THE PROBLEM OF EVIL

Open and relational theology answers our biggest questions about God and life. It doesn't tell us to shut off our brains, play mystery cards when backed into conceptual corners, or claim God is entirely incomprehensible. Those aren't real answers. No skyhook appeals to theological mumbo jumbo here.

Without believable answers to our biggest questions, some people will adopt atheism. According to polls, the problem of evil is the primary reason atheists do not believe. "If a loving and powerful God exists," they ask, "why doesn't He prevent genuine evil?"

Good question!

Open and relational theology offers a credible answer. Not a side-stepping deflection or "we'll just have to wait 'til heaven to find out." In fact, more people initially embrace open and relational theology for its solution to questions of evil than for any other reason.

We've already seen that God, as understood by open and relational thinkers, does not cause harm, negligence, or abuse. God didn't create the universe foreknowing every rape and torture, which would mean these evils were inevitable. A God who plans or even permits evil doesn't love perfectly. You can't trust Him. The inability of conventional theologies to explain evil is a good reason to reject them.

The solution that open and relational thinkers offer comes in various forms. I won't try to summarize them all, but generally they say God doesn't cause evil or control others. And God doesn't permit evil for some greater good.

Consequently, the open and relational God isn't guilty of failing to stop the pointless pain and unnecessary suffering we endure. You can see this logic from what we've said about this God's power.

SOLVING THE PROBLEM

Let me be more specific. Below are five ideas widely embraced by open and relational thinkers. Together, they solve the problem of evil. For details, see my book *God Can't: How to Believe in God and Love after Tragedy, Abuse, and Other Evils.*[5]

Not *every* open and relational thinker agrees with each idea. Nor do all use the language I do. But these ideas have wide acceptance in the open and relational community, no matter how they are expressed.

First, God's love is self-giving, others-empowering, and therefore uncontrolling. Because God loves everyone and everything in every moment, God *can't* control others. To put it in relational terms: a relational God of uncontrolling love can't singlehandedly prevent evil done by free creatures, smaller organisms, or inanimate sources. A loving God without the ability to control can't be rightly blamed for causing or allowing evil.

God can't prevent evil singlehandedly.

Second, a relational God suffers with the harmed and hurting. Rather than aloof and unconcerned, God feels our pain immediately after we do. Although without tear ducts, God metaphorically cries when we cry and literally feels sorrow. Those who suffer have God as a fellow-sufferer who understands.[6]

God suffers with us.

Third, God responds to hurt by trying to heal. God works at the smallest and simplest levels of our bodies and creation. God works with conscious agents, social organizations, and civilizations too. To say God "works to heal" does not mean God singlehandedly fixes us. Creatures and creation must play a role for the healing process to be successful. Without cooperation, healing is impossible.

God works with us to heal.

Fourth, God squeezes whatever good can be squeezed from the bad God didn't want in the first place. Evil is not part of a divine master plan. God doesn't send pointless pain to teach us a lesson, build our character, or micromanage creation for some greater good. But God works with us moment by moment to create beauty from ashes. Any good that follows evil has God as its inspiration and creatures or creation as contributors.

God works to wring good from bad.

Finally, God calls creatures and creation to join the work to overcome evil. Although unable to stop evil singlehandedly, God can stop it when we or others cooperate with the divine work of love. The Creator needs creation's partnership. Our lives are significant, in part, because we make an essential difference in God's ongoing endeavors to overcome evil with good.

God needs our cooperation.

Most who encounter these ideas have questions. While intuitive, each idea opposes aspects of conventional theologies we've been taught. Fortunately, open and relational thinkers give good answers to those questions. Find them in other open and relational writings or in my book *Questions and Answers for God Can't*.[7]

AMIPOTENCE ANSWERS QUESTIONS

The positive implications of embracing the idea of amipotence are wide ranging.

It solves the traditional problem of evil, as we've just seen, and that's a big deal. It helps us understand divine revelation, including scriptural errors and diverse interpretations. Saying God's love is uncontrolling helps make sense of why there are so many religions, with us not needing to label others as "deceived by Satan" or as ignorant when they understand God differently than we do. It helps us understand why prayers aren't always answered or miracles don't always occur.

Amipotence helps us understand why God doesn't prevent climate change singlehandedly (God literally can't), doesn't write messages in the clouds to prove God's existence (again, God can't), doesn't guarantee that the most qualified people get elected to political office (God can't), and so on.

God's amipotence answers so many questions!

GOD IS STRONGER

Let's return to Gracie.

In the story about freeing a car stuck in snow, Gracie was the most powerful. Using her voice, she persuaded others to use their bodies for good. Perhaps you now understand why God is powerfully persuasive too.

God is far, far stronger than Gracie, however. She is only in one place when influencing. An omnipresent God influences all creatures and creation, including the smallest entities and the largest societies. Gracie persuaded in one moment, but God persuades constantly. While Gracie loves sometimes, but not always, God's amipotence *always* loves. Gracie's imagination of the possibilities is limited, but God knows all the possibilities of love in each moment and calls us to choose the best. And so on.

God is profoundly more powerful than you or me or creation. And yet God is uncontrolling.

Of course, Gracie's relatives could have ignored her. Most of us prefer watching the Cowboys lose to pushing cars in the snow. We can ignore God too. I know I have, and I suspect that's true of everyone. We've all failed to respond to God's calls.

But many *do* respond to God's beckoning. When we witness beauty, compassion, design, cooperation, excellence, and whatever is good, we witness creatures and creation responding well to a good God. It's co-operation, co-laboring.

That's how open and relational theologians think about God's power. Not everyone embracing the label uses my language. But all say we should scrap conventional views of divine power if we want to answer our biggest questions, especially questions about evil.

Rethinking God's power can make a loving difference.

QUESTIONS:

1. How important is freedom in your theology? Can you make sense of life and moral responsibility if we are not free?
2. Do you think other creatures are free? Dogs? Mice? Amoebae? What are the implications of thinking nonhuman creatures are free?
3. What are the advantages and disadvantages of thinking God is like a loving parent?
4. If God always loves everyone and everything, how do we reconcile the evil in the world and our lives?
5. What are some implications of believing God is powerful but not controlling? How does the uncontrolling view help us make sense of things?

Scan the QR code for a video lecture on God and evil - Ian Ramsey Centre and Blackfriar's College, Oxford University.

5

PRESENT

In the minds of many, the word Creator = God. The two are synonymous. When "it's time to meet your Maker," we envision dying and encountering God in the afterlife.

Open and relational thinkers believe God creates. But they explain creating differently than conventional theologians. They think creatures and creation create too.

Created creatures co-create with their Creator.

CREATED CO-CREATORS

Once we consider this idea, it's obvious, because we see it in the world. I hike the backcountry of Idaho and often see creeks dammed by beavers. Using huge teeth, they saw down trees and branches to make homes across creeks. Inside these arbor-designed mounds, hidden from predators and backpackers like me, is a cavern made by these rodents of unusual size.

Beavers are just one species in the "creatures who create" domain. Birds make nests, bears make dens, squirrels make dreys, even salmon create spaces in creek beds to lay and fertilize their eggs. All animals create. Insects do too. I marvel at the creative abilities of wasps, ants, and beetles. If we broaden our view of "create" to all actions that influence others, *all* creatures create.

And there's sex, of course. Reproduction is creating. When an eight-year-old asks where she came from, parents say, "When mommy and daddy put their bodies together in a special way, you started growing in mommy's tummy. Nine months later, you were born."

Creation!

CREATOR

In what sense is God our Creator?

Some answer by saying God launched life long ago, but now creatures do all the work. After a creative burst, God sits on the clouds watching us work things out. "You take it from here," God says. "Good luck building the world!"

Few, if any, open and relational believers think God once created but now sips margaritas in retirement. They also reject the idea that God does *all* the creating. God's neither a do-nothing spectator who won't lift a finger nor an obsessive perfectionist who just wants it all His way.

So, what is God's creative activity?

A common open and relational answer says God acts to empower, inspire, and lure others in each moment. This is constructive activity on God's part, because it makes a real difference to creation. As creatures respond, their actions are creative too. God may suggest ideas, call for actions, nudge toward possibilities, entice toward beauty, convince it's time to tear down for a rebuild, and more.

God's creating varies, based on the actors, factors, and possibilities in each context.

Much of conventional theology sees God's creating like a mechanic building from pre-manufactured parts. Each inanimate bit is not alive, so this machine-in-the-making offers no responses. By contrast, open and relational thinkers see God's continual creating more like a gardener or community builder. Animated creation and creatures take part in the creative process God guides.

Using philosophical language, we might say God is a necessary cause in the moment-by-moment emergence of all things, but not the *only* cause. Just as our minds creatively influence but do not control our bodies, so God creatively influences but does not control the universe.

Creatures may follow the proposals of the Master Builder/ Gardener. But they might also veer off on destructive detours, going rogue in ruinous ways. Creation blossoms when creatures cooperate with constructive guidance. Evil, ugliness, and harm occur when they don't. In whatever way they respond, the Master Builder/Gardener adjusts moment by moment, drawing up new plans as needed, with the goal of a more diverse, healthy, and beautiful universe.

Open and relational thinkers credit God's creative activity for the differences and similarities we see. Divine creating is generatively diverse and wildly imaginative. But the world is not the product of God alone. The beauty of diversity is a joint venture.

In sum, God continually creates alongside creatures and creation who create in response.

WHEN GOD CREATES

There is no consensus among open and relational thinkers about *when* God started creating. Some believe God once existed alone and decided to create the universe out of nothing. The Latin phrase for this view is *creatio ex nihilo*. Most who affirm this idea say love motivated God's initial and ongoing creating.[1]

Others think God has *always* been creating. God never *started* as if there was an absolute beginning before which nothing existed. These thinkers say God constantly creates from or alongside creaturely others. Those "others" may be tiny and basic, or they may be large and complex. Many in this camp also think love motivates God's everlasting creating.

Most open and relational thinkers believe the scientific consensus that our universe is billions of years old. They affirm the development of complex life through a lengthy evolutionary process. But they say this process involves more than chance, genetic mutations, and natural selection. Creatures respond to their environments in self-organizing and self-causal ways. Symbiotic relations emerge and ideas pass through cultural forces that influence evolution's course. And God works in the process as a real creating contributor.

Evolution involves a variety of causal mechanisms.

PRO-SCIENCE

Open and relational thinkers embrace science but don't worship it. They're pro-science, because they take life seriously. The sciences are the most comprehensive activities we have to account for the evidence of existence. We ignore science at our peril.

Much of contemporary science takes as obvious the reality of ongoing time. This includes scientific assumptions about cause and effect, which imply a sequence of before and after. Scientists say life, new species, ecosystems, and new societies emerge over time. We live in an emerging and dynamic world, the world that open and relational thinkers take seriously when doing theology.

The godfather of contemporary science-and-religion dialogue is an open and relational thinker named Ian Barbour. His most influential book, *Religion in an Age of Science*, lays out four ways science and religion might relate. Barbour says the best way to make sense of reality integrates theology and science.[2] Open and relational physicist-priest John Polkinghorne and evolutionist-theologian Ilia Delio agree, as do many others.

Polkinghorne connects the universe of ongoing time with the God who experiences. "A world characterized by sequential becoming is appropriate to consider as a world of intrinsic temporality," says Polkinghorne. And "temporal knowledge implies a true divine engagement with unfolding time."

Integrating theology and science goes beyond noting their similarities and differences. It means adjusting theology in light of what science shows to be true and adjusting science to what theology argues as true. This integrative work isn't always easy, of course. But a look at the science-and-religion dialogue — past and present — shows open and relational scholars leading the research of what's best in science and theology.

CARING FOR CREATION

If we take seriously our role as co-creators with our Creator, we will live in particular ways. We no longer see ourselves as passive observers, drifting along without contributing to the world. No longer do we accept harmful practices in land management and animal care, for instance. No longer do we sit paralyzed as climate change alters our world for the worse. And so on.

As co-creators, our actions make a real difference.

How we treat one another, other species, and the earth matters. Those who do not cooperate with God's loving purposes undermine creation's well-being. The health of wild places around the world, for instance, depends on how we protect them.

I was reminded of being a created co-creator on a recent trip in Idaho's wilderness. I entered a valley decimated by strip mining. The stream once running through it now coagulated as a hodge-podge of ponds isolated by mounds of machine-excavated rock. Most trees had disappeared, and the now acidic soil prevented regrowth. The pond water sat murky decades after the mining mayhem.

The beavers I love cannot build their homes in this violated valley. Their absence affects the fish and other animals. The few trees that remain cannot support a bird population necessary for thriving ecosystems.

Human destruction has consequences.

What I witnessed is replicated in millions of ways around the globe. We're all affected by environmental degradation, even when we don't see the destruction. My friends of the forest — the birds, bears, and beavers — are dwindling. The salmon no longer spawn as they once did.

I tried to free a coyote recently. He was not wanted in land now grazed by cattle. A trap's jaws clasped his leg tightly, and I struggled to release him. He stared in shock as I worked six inches from his trembling muzzle. I talked in quiet and friendly tones, but also cried in frustration at my failure to release him.

I returned an hour later to find the trap empty, and a trapper's tracks showing my wild friend's life was snuffed out. Idaho laws consider me a criminal for trying to free my coyote companion. I'd rather be an outlaw of love than comply with decrees of death.

I often ask, "What can I do to make this world a better place for my animal friends?" Many today are asking this question. The majority in the open and relational community take concrete action to help the earth and its inhabitants, even if there's sometimes disagreement on what actions are best. My friends at the Institute for Ecological Civilization, for instance, are helping us to live well as co-creators, among other co-creators.

The God of open and relational theology cares about all creatures. I care too. And I commit to cooperating with this Creator for the good of all.

ARTIST AND MUSE

Open and relational theology's view of co-creating aligns with a phenomenon artists have witnessed for millennia. Many say a creative muse inspires their artistic endeavors. Others appeal to an unconscious source or goddess of ingenuity. William Blake called it "Imagination;" others call it the "Holy Spirit." No matter the label, creative artists often feel inspired by something beyond themselves.

As I write this book, I feel a kaleidoscope of factors and forces at play. Sometimes, I think God plays a leading role. Other times, my subconscious sits in the driver's seat. Sometimes I sense a force neither human nor divine but primal — a vitality, energy, or urge at the basis of reality.

As a photographer, I dance with a creative muse. Responding to the light, leading lines, and objects before me, I ponder my photo's composition and emotional tone. Then I click the shutter. As I make art, I wrestle with what pleases me and what might please others, influenced by forces beyond my control. This dance seems in some sense holy as I feel my way toward beauty.

I'm not saying my art comes entirely from a muse, entirely from me, or entirely from God. I don't want to blame God when my art is far from a masterpiece! And I make choices as an artist; I'm not a robot. Other factors and forces seem at work beside God and me, some of which rouse aesthetic inclinations I can't fully explain.

Many people talk about God as an artist, craftsman, or architect. William Blake called God the "poetic genius" and

Alfred North Whitehead said God is the "poet of the world." Today, some open and relational thinkers engage in what is called "theopoetics," a practice which uses artistic media and language to reflect on the Artist who cannot be fully understood.

Because it affirms the reality of God and creativity in a universe feeling its way into an undecided future, open and relational theology offers an ideal framework to make sense of art, artists, and the creative process. Art makes sense in a world emerging alongside a creative Artist and creaturely artists who feel about for ideas, forms, and images, inspired by what's possible.

Art moves the heart of this theology.

GOD PERCEIVES

"Does God watch when we're having sex?"

A friend posed this question to a Facebook group, and it inspired intriguing discussion. Some thought the question portrayed God as a pervert. Others said God watches everyone all the time, like the all-seeing eye on a dollar bill. Some said God *could* watch but chooses not to, respecting privacy or taking care of more important business, like making sure people pay their taxes. Some called the thought experiment "icky!"

An open and relational professor answered the question decades earlier. In her view, God feels the emotional tones of all our experiences, including sexual ones. When feeling the emotions sparked by great sex, God responds, "Thank you very much!"

I like her answer.

Asking if God watches sex might imply God perceives creation through sight. "Watch" suggests God has eyeballs and observes from a distance, like a peeping Tom. It assumes space between Creator and creation: God is "over there" and we're "over here."

Open and relational thinkers say God perceives everything, because God is directly present *to* everything. As an experiencer, God feels rather than sees. Creatures influence God, because divine perception comes through direct contact.

To put it another way, God knowing all that's knowable doesn't come because God is a detached mind outside space and time. An omnipresent God experiences creation in each moment and knows all that happens through immediate experience.

God is with us, not just in Jesus or during a religious experience, but at all times.

PANENTHEISM

If we polled open and relational thinkers, I suspect many would say the second most important divine attribute (after love) is God's universal and experiential presence. Let's connect God's relationality, which we explored earlier, with God's omnipresence.

Open and relational believers think God is present to and relates with all creation. Many call this "panentheism," which means "all *in* God."[3] It differs from both pantheism, which says, "all *is* God," and conventional theology, which says "nothing is in God." Scholars have teased out the implications of panentheism, and there is no consensus about all that it entails. At one academic conference, I noted more than a dozen meanings given the word![4]

At stake is what we mean by *in*. What does it mean for all creatures — from the simplest to most complex — and for all creation — including quarks and inanimate objects — to be "in" God?

Perhaps the best answer begins with an analogy.

My wife stands atop the list of people who have influenced me. Below her are my parents, children, and siblings. Also included on this list of influencers are friends and foes, co-workers and critics, leaders and losers, former girlfriends, and inspirational role models. Seattle Seahawks quarterback Jim Zorn influenced me positively as a kid, as did his teammate Steve Largent.

My list includes animals too. And the places I've lived, teams I've been on, and communities of which I've been part. I'd include the country in which I've lived, although I've visited every continent except Antarctica. A comprehensive list of influencers would include microbial, cells, germs, air, water, temperatures, weather, foods, and much more.

And God. I think God influences me every moment of my existence. An omnipresent and omni-influential God profoundly affects me, even when I'm unaware of it.

WE ARE EXPERIENTIAL

I mention my list to acknowledge the people, creatures, events, systems, God, and more who are "in" me. You won't find them sitting on couches in my heart or playing pickup basketball in my bladder. They're in my *experience*.

We're all experiential. Our lives, bodies, and world are a series of experiences. I don't mean we're disconnected from physical reality. Experiences have a physical dimension. Nor do I mean existence is merely a mind game. But experiences have a mental dimension too.[5]

We live moment by moment as beings composed of experiences with material and mental dimensions.

God is also experiential. God has a series of life experiences, an *everlasting* series. God's history doesn't have a beginning and never ends. And as experiential, others influence God.

That's how creation is "in" God. Panentheism says *all* creatures and creation — not just people — influence each moment of God's everlasting life. We're all in God's experience!

Let me dwell on the "all" aspect. Some who embrace relational theology say people are in God's experience. We are made in God's image, they'll say, and we have scriptural evidence that people influence God. Other relational theologians will add elephants, lions, dolphins, dogs, and the reddish-blond cat that roams my neighborhood. A few will add worms, insects, and maybe amoebae as part of God's experience.

But panentheism says *all* existing things and agents are in God's experience. All means *all*.

IN BUT NOT IDENTICAL TO

By "in," I don't mean God is a huge trash receptacle into which creation was dumped. Nor is God an egg inside of which we live independently from divine influence. Those are spatial analogies for being "in" God. I'm talking about the experiential meaning of "in."

God's also not an ocean into which droplets fall and lose all distinctiveness. Nor is God a bonfire enveloping all other flames. This isn't a fusion of creatures and Creator that collapses creaturely identities. That's pantheism.

Panentheism rejects the idea that you, me, and the universe *are* God. Distinctions between Creator and creature remain. We are *in* God's experience, but not identical to God.

Critics of panentheism sometimes say if we are in the divine experience, God must sin when we do. God lusts when people lust or kills when hyenas kill. They say a panentheistic God must cheat when we cheat. And so on. They think a God affected by creatures can't be morally perfect, steadfastly loving, or set apart as holy.

Open and relational panentheists point critics to the idea of God's essence-experience binate or divine dipolarity to overcome these criticisms. We explored those ideas earlier. God's essence is unchangingly secure while God's experience changes in relationship. Creatures can be in the divine experience without altering the divine nature. Creaturely sin — lust, killing, cheating, and more — can affect God's experience without altering God's perfect love.

The implications of panentheism are wide ranging. When conscious of its truths, I look at and live in the world differently. Panentheism prompts in me a sense of loving wonder at how God is present in and affected by everything.

Creator and creation relationally entangle, while retaining their differences and distinctiveness.

CONVENTIONAL ATONEMENT

A meme shows Jesus knocking on a door.

"Who's there?" says a voice behind the door.

"It's Jesus. Let me in."

"Why?"

"I need to save you."

"From what?"

"From what I'm going to do to you if you don't let me in!"

Another meme has Jesus talking to the reader: "I created humans able to be tempted to sin, created a tempting tree and a tempting serpent. Then, I killed nearly every creature with a flood because humans did what I made them able to do: sin. Later, I impregnated a woman with myself as her child, so that I could sacrifice myself to myself to save you from myself. Somebody had to die, because I'm angry that you do what I created you able to do: sin."

These memes represent how some conventional theologies portray salvation. The logic is so twisted we have to laugh. But such portrayals aren't actually funny and have led to real tears. And even death.

Some theologies add the element of free will to explanations of salvation. The results are largely the same: God set up the system, beats the hell out of the freely disobedient, takes the beating himself from himself, but sends to eternal torment anyone who doesn't freely accept Him.

Divinity discombobulated.

SALVATION

Open and relational theology thinks about salvation differently. Some of that difference comes when we shift the focus from what happens after death to how we live today. Instead of "pie in the sky, by and by," it's "love on the ground and all around."

As a Christian who thinks about salvation, my mind often goes to a Bible verse that says, "work out your salvation."[6] This text and others point to the role we play in enjoying the salvation God offers. The good life isn't divinely imposed.

To "work out your salvation" doesn't mean we do all the work. We don't save ourselves singlehandedly. It's not "if it's to be, it's up to me." God acts first to empower, inspire, and call. Cooperation is possible, according to the next lines of that passage, because God is "working in" us to encourage us "to want and to act" for good.[7]

Salvation is relational.

ATTUNEMENT

In Christian circles, these discussions often turn to what theologians call "theories of atonement." Over the millennia, believers have offered various atonement proposals. Most receive strong criticism today.

No single view of atonement is embraced by all open and relational thinkers. But particular themes fit open and relational intuitions.

Theories that promote God's steadfast love fit, for instance, while those that imply God is unloving, wrathful, or needs to kill, don't. God isn't a tyrant to be appeased or chief needing the blood of virgins.

It's also common for open and relational thinkers to affirm a necessary role for creatures in atonement. We are not passive pawns in a cosmic chess match. Nor are we slaves on the auction block available to the highest metaphysical bidder. Our choices count, our lives matter.

Atonement from an open and relational perspective is less about transactions and more about transformations. It's about becoming consistent lovers, not about paying a price. Atonement is less about meeting legal requirements and more about promoting genuine flourishing.

Open and relational thinkers also think big when it comes to atonement. God doesn't pre-decide that some people go to heaven and others roast in hell. All are invited to a loving relationship. No one is irredeemable. God cares about saving animals and creation too, because God loves everyone and everything.

Atonement involves attunement: attuning to God's love and responding accordingly.

EXPANSIVE SALVATION

From what are we saved?

A full answer would require multiple books, podcasts, articles, conversations, blog essays, speeches, and more. Because salvation can occur here and now and because we all need to be transformed, listing every way God works to save might be impossible.

Here's a list of fifteen ways God works to save...

God works to save us from our addictions and destructive habits.

God helps us to find a balance between work and play, rest and activity.

God invites us to experience meaningful relationships.

God calls us to stop acting in ways that hurt others.

God seeks to liberate the oppressed and include the marginalized.

God calls us to love ourselves well, including practicing self-care.

God seeks to enlighten the uneducated and foolish.

God wants to feed the hungry and raise us from debilitating poverty.

God encourages therapeutic processes by working to heal our bodies and psychoses.

God invites us to forgive and, where possible, reconcile.

God works to draw us away from a consumption mentality.

God works for the good of animals, plants, and other creatures.

God calls us to right relationships with lifelong partners and families.

God empowers us to love our enemies and help strangers.

God works to establish loving societies and civilizations.

This partial list suggests salvation not only includes but extends far beyond the individual. It's also communal, societal, even creation wide.

From an open and relational perspective, salvation is expansive. And it comes through relational love.

SEPARATED?

While in college, I was active in Campus Crusade for Christ, an evangelical organization committed to evangelism. This was before the group changed its name to "CRU" and before I learned about the horrors of medieval crusades. My purpose was to convince people to accept Jesus so they could go to heaven and avoid hell.

Crusade's primary witnessing tool is "The Four Spiritual Laws." The second law says, "Sin separates us from God." The accompanying graphic shows God on one side of a chasm — labeled "your sin" — and a person standing on the other.

The statement and image imply that a holy God can't be in the presence of unholiness. Sin separates us from God's love. Jesus must do something — die on a cross — to bridge the chasm.

To say we're separated from God suggests both spatial and relational distance. A pure God keeps His distance over there while impure sinners stand sullied over here. God cannot relate to the vile and shameful. But thanks to Jesus' death, God can bear to look at us... if we accept what Jesus has done. Those who don't accept have real estate in hell awaiting them.

This view of salvation makes no sense to me now.

We can't be spatially separated from a God who is omnipresent. That's impossible. And an open and relational God perpetually gives and receives in relation with us. There's no relational separation.

Let me recommend a better way to think about sin: the impairing of relationships. We're always related to and loved by God, but sin sabotages our well-being and the well-being of others. Like an estranged couple who remain married but have big-time issues, our sin estranges us from the Greatest Lover of All.

We do the estranging, not God. God's mind doesn't need to be changed about us. God's mind is set: God will always relate with and love us. That's guaranteed. We need to change our minds (and actions) about God. And about ourselves and others.

TURNING POINTS

Many of us identify important moments — turning points — in our spiritual journeys. One comes when we realize God loves us personally and fully. We are God's beloved! We remind ourselves of this often, so it will sink in and transform us. Accepting God's love is fundamental to salvation.

Another turning point comes when we realize divine love extends to everyone, even our enemies, and to everything, even the last and least. We are *all* God's beloved! This changes how we treat others. We appreciate them, befriend them, respect them, and forgive them when they harm us or others. We see others as cherished by God and valuable.

A third turning point comes when we orient our lives around love. We commit to living lives of love. This involves continual recommitting, of course, because we move moment by moment through life, facing new opportunities and challenges. The life of love is an adventure.

Salvation is a process. We're saved in one moment and can be saved again in the next. Salvation always involves God acting first on our behalf and then our response to God and others.

HOPE IS A VERB

Open and relational thinkers talk about hope differently than those who embrace conventional theologies. For starters, open and relational thinkers consider hope a verb, not a fixed and predetermined state. We choose to hope when we live in step with the Ultimate Agent of hope.

We hope.

Part of hoping comes as God calls us to something new in each moment. The past doesn't settle our future. We're not stuck indefinitely or entirely determined by what's happened. Life is not *Groundhog Day* in perpetuity.

No matter what we've done, or others have done to us, God invites us to what's best in the next moment, given what's possible. Something novel awaits. While not just anything is workable, more is possible than we think or imagine.

Sometimes hope sneaks up on us.

This hope isn't automatic, in the sense that things will inevitably work out well. Open and relational hope doesn't cross its fingers, close its eyes, and believe things will magically turn out right. We and others have a role to play. We act in hope by cooperating with a God of hope.

Hope acts.

OBJECTIVE IMMORTALITY

What most open and relational thinkers mean by "hope" and "salvation" is not limited to the next moment or even to this life. Most of us expect continuing experiences in an afterlife. But some don't. Before looking at the majority view, let's look at the minority.

What if this life is all we have? Would our lives matter? Could it satisfy us living and dying on the third rock from the sun?

Some open and relational thinkers believe immortality consists only of what we do before we die. We are immortal, according to this view, because our lives contribute to God's everlasting work of transformation. These contributions persist beyond our mortality in the divine mind.

From this perspective, our lives matter in the future, because God builds from our present actions after we're dead and gone. This view is often called "objective immortality," because our lives make an objective difference to God's work after we perish.

SUBJECTIVE IMMORTALITY

Most open and relational thinkers believe we make an objective difference to God, but they also think we continue experiencing after our hearts stop beating. This view says we maintain awareness after death and is called "subjective immortality." The word "subjective" doesn't mean, "it all depends on how you look at it." It means we are experiencing subjects, interacting with others.

What we will experience in the afterlife is, of course, almost entirely in the realm of speculation. We just don't know. But our speculation should be shaped by what we believe about God and the structures of existence.

I know of no open and relational thinker who believes God sends people to eternal conscious torment. In other words, they reject the traditional idea of hell. The idea that God sends people to eternal punishment not only contradicts steadfast love, it also has little if any scriptural support.

Some open and relational thinkers believe God brings everyone into everlasting bliss. This view is called "universalism," and it says a loving God carries everyone to heavenly happiness after they die. As kids might say it, "Allee, Allee, in come free!"

Others say most people aren't ready to live right for eternity. Those "not ready" need to grow in love before entering paradise. This is the view traditionally called purgatory, although it has many versions. We need an overhaul to enjoy eternal bliss.

Still others believe some people will continually refuse to cooperate with God. These unrepentant fools freely refuse divine grace. God doesn't send such people to eternal hell. Instead, they are annihilated. They stop existing.

RELENTLESS LOVE

I call my view of the afterlife "relentless love." Like most open and relational thinkers, I believe in life after death. I think we continue experiencing long after our bones turn to dust, and our flesh becomes food for flowers.

The relentless love view says God always loves everyone, never giving up on anyone. By "always," I mean without end: "Always" with a capital A! God everlastingly invites creatures to relationships of love in this life and the next. That includes everyone who considers themselves enemies of God. Even God's love for enemies is relentless.

Although God always loves, we can reject God's invitations. When we do, we suffer the *natural* negative consequences that come from saying no to the positive power of love. God doesn't exact revenge when we reject love. We don't get a divine spanking, nor are we annihilated. God always invites, calls, and woos us toward well-being.

God's love never gives up and always hopes.[8]

Theoretically, some people, even in the afterlife, may never say "yes" to God. But the steadfast love of God continues inviting them, moment by moment, everlastingly. Consequently, the idea of relentless love provides plausible grounds to believe all will *eventually* cooperate. This hope, that God's love will finally convince every creature to embrace the invitation to well-being, comes from amipotence, not omnipotence.

That's relentless love in a nutshell.[9]

QUESTIONS:

1. What do you think of the idea you and all creation are in God's experience (panentheism)?
2. Does the idea that we co-create with our Creator make sense? Does it make you cringe or excite you? What are some of its implications?
3. What does it mean to believe God saves as we and creation cooperate?
4. What role does love play in your view of salvation? Can we be saved if we do not love? Can God save in an unloving way?
5. What are your thoughts on the afterlife?

Scan the QR code for a video lecture on panentheism - Munich School of Philosophy.

6

LOVING

I conclude with a personal chapter.

The previous chapters have also been personal, in the sense that I explain open and relational theology from my own perspective. I interspersed a few of my proposals too when I thought appropriate.

But in this chapter, I play my ace.

I earlier listed reasons many embrace open and relational theology. Those reasons point to its usefulness, truthfulness, experiential fit, consonance with scripture, alignment with science, and more. I embrace them all. But the biggest reason I adopt open and relational theology is...

LOVE!

In my opinion, open and relational thought provides the best overall framework for understanding and promoting love. A conceptually clear and experientially adequate framework is important for people like me who think beliefs about God should be reasonable and account for the way we live. A good framework can even incline us to love more expansively and consistently.

Ideas matter.

A LOVE FRAMEWORK

My number one goal is to live a life of love. That goal gives purpose to my life. It's my primary intention.

Having a coherent love framework doesn't guarantee I'll *always* love. I try, but sometimes fail. But an adequate theology of love provides confidence that my aim to love makes sense in the grand scheme of things.

I wouldn't be motivated to love, for instance, if I thought I wasn't free. I'd just do what I thought was predetermined and assume my self-centeredness was pre-decided.

I wouldn't be motivated to prevent suffering if I thought God could do it singlehandedly. I'd assume the pain I encounter is part of a plan God designed. I'd assume victims get what they deserve.

I couldn't make sense of love—creaturely or divine—if my conceptual framework said it was not relational, which some conventional theologies claim. Love relationships are real.

I couldn't love if I thought values were illusions and the categories of better and worse were entirely my preference. That's extreme relativism, and love makes no sense without values.

I couldn't love a God who sends people to eternal torment. It wouldn't make sense to love those I thought God was sending there. If God wants them to suffer forever, so should I.

I doubt I'd care for creation if I thought God didn't care for it too. I might just let it burn, drown, and starve. Tough luck, world. And so on.

A love-based view of reality makes a difference to how you and I live. If love is the greatest, the ultimate, the highest aim of God and existence, we ought to embrace theologies that make sense of that preeminence. I believe open and relational theology makes sense of love's supremacy better than any other.

AGAPE

If you've spent much time in Christian circles, you've probably heard the word *agape*. What you might not know is that you have Anders Nygren to thank for the word's popularity. His 1930s book *Agape and Eros* made *agape* a household word, at least among Protestants. Nygren said *agape* is the unique form of Christian love and key to understanding God. Although few know his name today, Nygren's claims about *agape* have influenced tens if not hundreds of millions of people.

I first heard about *agape* in Sunday school. I was learning from the Bible, teachers, and my parents that God loves us all. Jesus said I ought to love God and others as myself. The love I felt called to express differed from love described by Billboard's Hot 100 or my love of ice cream. Having a special word—*agape*—made sense.

By my twenties, I was convinced good theology placed love at its center. I wasn't sure what that meant, so I started studying books and attending academic conferences. In that context, a professor recommended *Agape and Eros*, by then considered a classic book.[1]

On my first reading, I was confused. For one thing, Nygren claims New Testament *agape* differs radically from Old Testament love. This didn't mesh with how I interpreted the Bible, although I had plenty of questions about divine violence in the earlier scriptures. Nygren's radical split between Old and New Testaments made me uneasy.

Nygren tries to connect his *agape* view to Jesus. I say "tries," because the more I studied *Agape and Eros*, the less convinced I was by his arguments. Jesus' teachings and stories just didn't fit Nygren's proposals.

Nygren assumes humans are utterly depraved. We are also not free in his view, at least in any meaningful sense. He believes depraved creatures make no positive contributions to the work of love. We're tubes through which God passes love, like garden hoses through which water flows. Hoses are instruments, not partners. This view of the God-creature relationship clashes with biblical examples in which people act as God's relational partners. Even animals sometimes partner with God.

I came to believe Nygren's views had little connection with how biblical writers portray God. I later discovered his views prompt scholars of scripture to shake their heads in disagreement. Few biblical passages support his perspective.

By the time I reviewed *Agape and Eros* for my doctoral dissertation, I found little value in its pages. I now believe it's the worst academic book on love written in the 20th century.

A NARCISSIST

Nygren has a villain in *Agape and Eros,* and that villain is the early church father St. Augustine. According to Nygren, *agape* is God's love coming down to us, creating value where there is none. By contrast, Augustine believed we can love God as those drawn upward to what's valuable. Figuring the enemy of my enemy might be my friend, I turned to Augustine.

And I was disappointed! Love is not central to Augustine. His most extensive exploration of it comes in *Teaching Christianity.*[2] There he claims love has two forms: "use" and "enjoyment." We love God by enjoying Him because God is supremely valuable. We both use and enjoy creatures, although love for them never satisfies like love for God.

When Augustine applies his logic to God, disaster strikes. We discover God can't love us.

Can't!

A God who lacks nothing finds nothing in us to enjoy. So, God can't love by enjoying us. A fully independent deity does not depend on us and finds nothing in us useful. So, God doesn't love by using us either. For Augustine, God only loves himself.[3]

Augustine's God is a complete narcissist.

The very heart of how I understand the gospel — that God loves me, you, and all creation in the sense of wanting our salvation/well-being — collapses in Augustine's logic.

Augustine's theology has other problems too. So does Nygren's.[4] Many problems arise from misunderstandings each has about how scripture portrays love. Many derive from how we understand love in our own lives. Most of their problems come from failing to recognize God's love as relational, creatures as free and valuable, and the future as yet to be determined. Those ideas are indispensable to an adequate theology of love.

Nygren and Augustine represent what I came to reject in conventional theology.

LOVE ADVANTAGES

I could write page after page listing the advantages open and relational theology offers to understanding love. I have—in other books![5] But let me rapid-fire some below. I've touched on some of these ideas earlier; I introduce others.

An open and relational theology framework supports the idea that...

God loves everyone, every creature, and all creation. No exceptions. Conventional theologies say or imply God loves only "the chosen," "the righteous," or even just humans. Open and relational theology says the Great Lover of the Universe acts for the well-being of everyone and everything, and God values everyone and everything. This Lover wants creation to flourish.

Call this advantage, *unlimited love.*

God's love doesn't just give, it also receives. It's benevolent and empathetic. God responds to our ups and downs, pain and joy, confusion and clarity, dreams and failures. Open and relational theology portrays God as one who speaks *and* listens.[6] An adequate theology portrays love as relational giving and receiving. Conventional theologies portray God as not relating this way with creatures.

Call this advantage, *creative-responsive love.*[7]
God calls us to love in response. God invites cooperation, and our responses matter. The Wondrous One woos, the Great Proposer propositions. We can enter a love relationship in which our choices make a difference. Open and relational theology insists that creatures contribute to the work of love; many conventional theologies have no room for creaturely contributions.

Call this advantage, *cooperating love.*
If we fail to answer love's call, God doesn't retaliate. An open and relational God keeps no record of wrongs and condemns the payback of eye for an eye, a tooth for a tooth. Natural negative consequences come from saying no to love, but God doesn't dish out those consequences. They're naturally rendered within the situation. Unlike the God of many conventional theologies, the Faithful Forgiver in open and relational thought doesn't run a retribution racket.

Call this advantage, *forgiving love.*
An open and relational God feels compassion. We get hurt, are confused, and wrestle with addictions. God cares. Sometimes we hurt others on purpose and other times accidentally. God weeps. Whether we are inflicting pain as perpetrators or suffering from it as victims, God hurts with us. The compassionate God of open and relational theology suffers with everyone feeling pain. The conventional God doesn't—in fact, can't.

Call this advantage, *suffering love.*
We each have intuitions about the values inherent in love. But conventional theologies say we can't trust those intuitions, because we're hopelessly warped and twisted. By contrast, open and relational theology says our perception of value tells

us something true about God and reality, and we ought to live in light of those values.

Call this advantage, *intuiting love.*

God's actions provide examples of what love entails. We see it expressed in Jesus and others, as they weep with those who weep, turn the other cheek, or go the extra mile. Conventional theologies portray God's love as essentially different from ours, making it impossible for us to love like God does. Open and relational thought says divine love isn't an exception to the fundamental framework of what counts as loving. Therefore, we can imitate God.[8]

Call this advantage, *imitating love.*

God's unchanging nature is love. We can trust God to love, because love *is* what God does. It's God's heart, to use common language. To put it philosophically, God necessarily loves, because love comes logically first among divine attributes. To put it as a double negative and annoy English teachers, God cannot *not* love. Many conventional theologies say God could stop loving us and sometimes does, but open and relational theology says God *must* love.

Call this advantage, *loving by nature.*

An open and relational God doesn't cause or allow evil. God's not orchestrating a predetermined plan to perpetrate or even permit pointless pain. The Great Lover's power is self-giving and others-empowering, so it can't singlehandedly decide outcomes. This God isn't in control — Thank God! — unlike the deity that conventional theologies envision.

Call this advantage, *uncontrolling love.*

We can't imagine love without freedom. Open and relational theology says the future is open and not settled, so we freely choose to love or not. God can't force us, and nature doesn't determine us. Conventional theologies say God foreordains or foreknows, and both views undermine the basis for thinking that we love freely.[9]

Call this advantage, *freely loving*.

God never stops loving. In this life, the next, or ever. Not when we're doing well or doing badly; not when we're focusing on God or preoccupied with other things. Many conventional theologies say God gives up on some people, sending them to eternal torment or annihilating them. But nothing can separate us from the everlasting love of an open and relational God.[10]

Call this advantage, *relentless love*.

I could list more advantages this theology provides for understanding and living in love. But these should suffice for explaining why open and relational theology appeals to me. And why conventional theology does not.

For the sake of love, I'm open and relational.

SELF-LOVE

An open and relational theology supports the conviction that love seeks the common good. That's another way of saying love wants the well-being of all creation and God.

My own well-being is part of the good of the whole. This means I should take care of myself, because self-love promotes the common good. Open and relational theology provides a conceptual basis not only for loving God and others, but also for loving oneself.

Self-love takes various forms. I set goals to eat healthy foods, exercise regularly, and get sufficient rest, although I sometimes fail miserably to meet them. Spending time in nature is an important form of self-love for me. I like to hike the remote Owyhees, a sparsely populated region spanning Idaho, Oregon, Nevada, and California. For me, self-love means watching thought-provoking movies with my wife at The Flicks and other theaters. We try to see each Oscar-nominated feature film before Hollywood announces the winners and watch every film with an Oscar-nominated actress or actor.

I try to balance the time I spend working and playing, but that's an ongoing effort. Too much work or play proves harmful. In fact, I don't decide to love myself in one moment and am thereafter assured I will always love myself. Each moment requires new decisions and new forms my love might take.

Unfortunately, many conventional theologies have no place for self-love. They equate self-love with selfishness, in the sense of always putting one's own good before the good of others. The Protestant theologian Martin Luther even considered self-love the quintessential sin. I believe self-love is vital to loving well; without it, we wither and fade. And if we don't love ourselves, we fail to love someone God loves: ourselves!

Open and relational theology says God *always* loves me. God's very nature is uncontrolling love, which means God *must* love me and *can't* control me. The Lover of All relationally entangles with us as individuals and with all creation, and this entangling is everlasting.

I like to put it this way: I can't stop God from loving me, because God's love is uncontrollable. But God can't control me, because God's love is uncontrolling.

FAITH AND LOVE

I've long appreciated a sentence written by the Apostle Paul: "The only thing that counts is faith expressing itself in love."[11] When he wrote this, Paul was responding to religious practices and beliefs that divided Jesus-followers in his day. He says active faith, when expressed rightly, prompts us to love.

It's easy to think "faith expressing itself in love" means we ought first to adopt a correct set of beliefs and then express them in a loving way. For Christians, this might mean affirming particular doctrines, ancient creeds, a "biblical theology," etc., and then graciously presenting these affirmations to others.

I endorse sharing beliefs in a loving manner. I've witnessed too many people expressing beliefs—especially on social media—in ways anything *but* loving. Sharing beliefs lovingly is obviously better than burning at the stake those with a different belief system.

But expressing one's beliefs lovingly is not enough. Bad theology expressed in a kind way is still bad theology.

Some seem to think expressing their beliefs in a loving way *proves* the superiority of those beliefs. "They will know we are Christians by our love" really means "See, we're right after all!" Love becomes an evangelism strategy.

Using love as a method to preach correct beliefs eventually wears thin. Many become disillusioned and leave faith communities. Sometimes the once faithful reflect on beliefs handed down and realize they make little sense. Other times, "orthodox" ideas clash with their deepest moral intuitions.

Sometimes conventional theological beliefs run headlong into truths in science, culture, or personal experience. "Correct beliefs" can even become fuel for hatred, which obviously opposes love.

Given the problems that emerge from putting correct beliefs before love, some people reject altogether the task of seeking correct beliefs. "It doesn't matter what you believe," they say, "it matters how you act." Or "I don't need beliefs, I just love."

The rejection of belief makes little sense. After all, the statement, "I don't need beliefs" is itself a belief. And those who say "it doesn't matter what you believe" usually *want* you to believe their view. The truth is we humans can't rid ourselves entirely of beliefs. We're believing creatures.

But there is a better way. And that way returns us to the priority of love.

If we switch the order of Paul's words, something revolutionary emerges. Instead of "faith expressing itself in love," let's try "love expressing itself in faith." This switch begins with love and then formulates beliefs in light of love.

Love becomes the guide.

This switch in order might be "six of one, half a dozen of the other." If our beliefs already center on love, expressing love seems natural. In that case, "faith expressing itself in love" also means "love expressing itself in faith." Six of one, half a dozen of the other.

Few conventional theologies focus on love, however, or let it be their guide. Most start with God's power, a sacred book, an ancient creed, particular religious experiences, or a doctrinal issue. Problems follow. Even though Jesus says love is the greatest command, Paul says the greatest of the virtues is love, and John says God *is* love, few theologies follow their lead.[12]

What if love were the starting point, through line, and destination? What if it were not just a method but also the message? What if love were the key to understanding God, how to live well together, and the nature of reality itself? What if love were both the center of simple theology and the motif scholars like me require to understand the complexities of God and existence?

If we make love theology's beginning, middle, and end, we arrive at beliefs common among open and relational thinkers. Core notions of love align with our deepest intuitions. Good theology is more than intuition, of course. A robust theology of love draws also from scriptures, wisdom traditions, sciences and arts, philosophies, personal experiences, culture, and practical living. It listens to the heart and works with the head.

Love expressing itself in faith.

JESUS

What I've been proposing fits well with how Jesus lived and spoke, celebrated and suffered. That's why I try to pattern my life after him. I want to love like Jesus loved.

I don't know if I admired Jesus because I first realized the priority of God's love or realized God is loving because I first admired Jesus. Chicken and egg, I guess. But I think Jesus best reveals the God whose nature and name is love.[13]

I probably don't need to list the *many* ways Jesus loved. Even people outside Christianity know something about this legendary lover from Nazareth. We see it in his teaching, forgiving, healing, guiding, warning, non-anxious presence; in his liberating, suffering, storytelling, listening, stillness, dying, and more. Just read a few Gospel chapters for examples.

Jesus' love is amazing!

As a young person, my faith involved having a personal relationship with Jesus. The relational element matched what I read in the Bible about God and what I sensed intuitively. This proved crucial as I maneuvered through life—sometimes well, sometimes poorly—as a young person.

I eventually discovered that many people speak about a personal relationship with Jesus but really mean he is their little buddy or good luck charm. They can count on this Jesus to support their political views and baseball teams. Some claim to receive personal messages from him, messages that make no sense to me. Many people have done evil in Jesus' name.

The electronic-music band Depeche Mode taught me that Jesus transcends anyone's pet project or personal ambition. Their song, "Personal Jesus," helped me realize I can't be a personal Jesus to my girlfriend, or her to me. Jesus doesn't cater to my every whim, and I'm not the Messiah.

Jesus is bigger than any agenda — except the agenda of love.

IMPERSONAL

As a twenty-something, I moved from A) a personal relationship with Jesus to B) skepticism about religion, to C) atheism, and then D) thinking God exists as an impersonal force. I could write an entire book on this process. For now, let me talk about why D was not my final stop.

I returned to belief, in part, because it made sense of creation's beauty, my moral intuitions, the religious experiences of people around the world, and the design of the universe. It also provided a ground for ultimate meaning.

After atheism, I at first believed God was a non-personal Depth, an amorphous Reality, or the Ground of Being. This transcendent Something didn't personally relate to me or interact with creation. The divine was just there, like the Force in Star Wars.

The problem is that theologies portraying God as impersonal do not support the idea of give-and-receive relations between God and the world. Or between me and God. I can act, pray, cry, or love, but a non-relational God can't respond. Even my sin and world's evil evoke nothing in Him.

As typically understood, the Ground of being is not relational. It just is. A non-personal Depth has no interactive attributes. An indistinct Reality is too vague to elicit my devotion. And none of these can love relationally.

An impersonal God can't relate to me, nor I to it.

A PET ROCK

I was seven when Greg Powers introduced me to pet rocks. Greg and I grew up with dogs, cats, and other animals. He was a step ahead with cultural trends, and he said kids were adopting rocks as pets.

We both laughed! To us, pets were creatures with whom we had relationships. We fed them, and they played with us. We cared for them, and they provided companionship. Our dogs got excited when we returned from school and journeyed with us on adventures. Our cats would purr and rub against our legs, desperate for a back scratching.

Pet rocks can't do those things. They sit on shelves and dust settles on them. We can admire rocks. We can talk at them, shine them, or paint them blue. But they have no feelings for us. They can't communicate or empathize, initiate or respond. We might play with rocks, but they don't play with us.

Pet rocks and an impersonal God share a lot in common. The two communicate the same way. They respond similarly and are equally compassionate. Rocks love as effectively as an impersonal God, and it makes as much sense to befriend a rock as a friendship-incapable God.

Many people think the best theology available after deconstruction from traditional faith says that God is non-relational. Some think rejecting naïve faith and adopting a sophisticated one requires rejecting a personal God.

Nonsense!

It doesn't help that many conventional theologies reinforce the myth God is not relational. But we don't have to swallow ideas popular in medieval times, especially when they contradict our experiences, the best ideas in philosophy and science, scripture, and so much more.

Open and relational theology provides a sophisticated conceptual scheme to affirm a personal relationship with a loving God. It rejects those aspects of naïve faith not worth keeping but keeps the idea that God gives and receives in ongoing relations. It fits the major themes of scripture, while harmonizing with fundamental ideas in contemporary science, philosophy, and the arts. Open and relational theology makes the best sense of what happens every day and of our deepest intuitions.

This theology best accounts for what I think is most important: love. If love is active, responsive, and promotes what's good, a theology that portrays God as active, responsive, and promoting good makes sense.

By contrast, the God of many conventional theologies is like a pet rock.

LOVE MISUNDERSTOOD

To make a point, let me pick on Augustine again. He may be the most influential conventional theologian and the most wrong about love. His ideas deserve criticism.

As I mentioned, Augustine's God only loves Himself. Augustine comes to this conclusion by following his logic that 1) God is alone supremely valuable and 2) to love is to desire what is valuable. Therefore, God desires what is supremely valuable: Himself.

Tragically, those ideas prevent Augustine from embracing what Jesus called the greatest commandments: Love God and love others as yourself.[14] To me, that's a monumental tragedy!

Here's what I mean...

Augustine thinks we love well when we enjoy what is supremely valuable. That's God. To love others and ourselves properly — beings not supremely valuable — means loving God *in* others and ourselves. Love for anything other than the supremely valuable would be misdirected and misguided. We properly love only as we love God.

I'd like you to do an exercise. Read the previous paragraph but replace "love" with the word "desire" every time it appears. You'll discover something profound but rarely noted even by scholars. Augustine thinks to love is to *desire*. Because of this misunderstanding, bad theology follows.[15]

As typically used in scripture and daily life, however, "love" means acting to help, being a blessing, doing good, benevolence, promoting well-being, and so on. Love involves intentional action as a relational response to do something beneficial.[16] This may or may not involve desire.

Love's primary aim is doing good.

Augustine presents us with two problems. 1) He doesn't understand love as promoting well-being, despite this being the primary way writers of scripture understand it. 2) He doesn't think God is relational, and it's impossible to understand love if it's not relational.

Consequently, Augustine can't say we love God and others as ourselves — the first and second commandments — and actually mean we do good to God, others, and ourselves. Because he thinks love is desire, the idea that love helps, blesses, or promotes well-being doesn't mesh with his theology.

GOD'S WELL-BEING

Now for the payoff:

Open and relational theology affirms our deep intuition that loving God and others as ourselves means we can promote the good of others, ourselves, and... God!

That's right, God's well-being is enhanced when we love.

This guy named Thomas Jay Oord, writing this book in the little-known state of Idaho, in the weirdly named town of Nampa, sitting on a half plastic, half steel chair, typing on an older model Surface Pro computer... actually influences the God of the universe!

To put it another way, open and relational theology makes sense of Jesus' first command to love God. We love God when we promote God's well-being. To use more biblical language, we can bless God. Because God is directly present to us and affected by what we do, we can please God. *Any* time!

Open and relational theology also makes sense of Jesus' second command, that we love others as ourselves when we seek to promote the well-being of others and ourselves. Because God is present to all creation and feels what occurs everywhere, our love for others promotes their well-being and God's. To put it another way, we can love others for their own good and affect God's good too. My granddaughter's joy increases when I take her for a walk along the greenbelt, for instance. As we walk, God's joy increases along with hers.

I can't get over how thrilled I am by this: we can enhance God's well-being!

MONICA, CHAD, AND JENNY

I began this book with five stories. Each asked big questions about God. In subsequent chapters, I offered answers open and relational theology provides. All of them, in one way or another, involve love.

Monica asked why God didn't stop her rape. Millions of sex-abuse survivors have asked that question or something similar. Add to them the questions countless people ask every day when they suffer needlessly. It would be safe to say *billions* of people wonder why God didn't prevent the abuse, tragedy, or harm they endure.

The usual responses are unconvincing. Some say God wants to teach us a lesson by causing or allowing tragedy or abuse. Others say evil is part of a divine plan, mysteriously working for some incomprehensible good. Some say those who suffer are being punished, getting what's due to them. And others simply appeal to mystery: God's ways are not our ways. If these were the only answers available, atheism would make better sense!

Some think they solve the problem by blaming evil on free will creatures. God "permits" evil, they say, instead of stopping the perpetrators. But we can't answer the questions Chad asked by appealing to free will. The Covid-19 pandemic is a natural evil apparently caused by no one's choice. A loving God capable of controlling viruses ought to have prevented the pandemic that took Jenny. She'd be alive if God had stopped the virus.

In previous pages, I've shown how open and relational theology provides believable answers to questions about unnecessary suffering. God didn't pre-decide everything, and God doesn't foreknow what will occur. The future is open, undetermined, and inherently unknowable.

I believe a loving God can't control anyone or anything. This open and relational belief plays a key role in solving the problem of evil. We can trust a loving God who neither causes nor permits pointless pain.

YOUR SUFFERING

The preceding paragraphs provide a theoretical solution to why God doesn't prevent evil. But for you, the reader, suffering is probably more than theory. It's personal.

Maybe you were groomed by a youth pastor and molested. Perhaps you suffered verbal and physical abuse from a parent, relative, teacher, or coach. Maybe you lost a child through miscarriage, disease, or accident. Perhaps you've suffered from a debilitating illness. Maybe cancer ravaged you or someone you love. Maybe you've been neglected or bullied for being different. Perhaps you suffer from lingering trauma caused by past horrors and heartache. Or something no one else knows or can imagine.

The "God can't" view is good news for you. An open and relational God loves you personally. You were not abandoned, punished, or being taught some lesson. Your suffering isn't from or even permitted by God.

God could not have singlehandedly stopped the harm you experienced but was present during your ordeal. God suffers when you suffer and works to squeeze whatever good can come from your pain. God *truly* cares.

Open and relational theology doesn't just answer abstract questions, as important as those are. It answers the personal questions you've been asking. And it says an uncontrolling God is always loving.

I'm sure you still have questions about how this works. That's natural. Open and relational thinkers respond to these questions with believable answers. See the resources I recommend at the conclusion of this book.

KYLER

Kyler seeks a meaningful way to live. He knows his actions don't matter if God foreordained or foreknows them. He won't raise his daughters to think their actions were predestined. Kyler wants a view of reality that affirms free will.

Open and relational theology affirms the reality of genuine but limited freedom. We are morally responsible beings who decide how to live moment by moment. Our free choices matter, and our lives count.

Some forms of open and relational theology say freedom, agency, and self-organization extend even to simple creatures and entities. The world is not a machine comprised of robots, large and small. It's a throbbing organism with dynamic creatures engaging one another in giving-and-receiving relations. Creation is alive.

If we're relational organisms in a relational world, relational love makes a whole lot of sense. It makes even more sense if a relational God acts as love's source, power, and urge. A world of organisms and relational God are essential ingredients in the recipe of love.

Kyler may not have a religious background, he may never become religious, and may not introduce his daughters to religion. But he *can* find meaning in love. He might find reasons to connect with others who seek to love, of course, and religious groups may help. But religious groups not oriented around love will hinder. He must choose wisely.

ROCHELLE

Rochelle realizes that petitionary prayer makes no sense if God knows the future. Asking God to do other than what will be done is like asking God to avoid creating the universe. A future that can be known with certainty is a settled situation, like the start of our universe is settled. There's no point in asking God to change a settled future.

An open and relational perspective provides a framework for understanding the prayers billions of people offer. Their prayers make a difference — to God, to the world, and to those who pray. The future will be different because of prayer, even though praying doesn't enable God to control others.

Love plays a role in prayer too. Most people pray wanting to help those in need: others or themselves. Helping behavior expresses love. Because we want a better future, we ask God for assistance.

When we pray with integrity, we also love ourselves. Prayers of integrity honor our intelligence and quest for truth. Open and relational theology doesn't ask us to pretend to believe in something we can't. We can follow Jesus' greatest command to love God with our minds when we pray with integrity.

Open and relational thinkers pray without crossing their fingers.

JIMMY

If the problem of evil is the primary reason some choose atheism, I suspect the problem of hell is the second. Jimmy is right: It makes no sense to believe a loving God would send someone to everlasting torment, even if she were rotten every day for a hundred years. The punishment doesn't fit the crime.

Of course, harmful consequences come—eventually—from harmful actions. Destructive choices hurt us, others, and the world. God always forgives wrongdoers, but we experience hell right now when we treat others and ourselves wrongly.

Open and relational theology admits the world has genuine goodness and genuine evil. It doesn't ask us to close our eyes to either. It also says actions have consequences. Jimmy and the guys around the campfire can believe in good and evil without believing a loving God damns anyone to everlasting torment.

The open and relational view provides hope for a better now and future. Guarantees of bliss could only come if God were controlling, but a God capable of control causes or permits evil here and now. Better to believe God empowers without overpowering, invites without repressing. And because God is everlastingly amipotent, love *can* win eventually... through persuasion.

Isn't that the way of love? "Love does not force its own way," to quote the Apostle Paul. "It never gives up and always hopes."[17] It's a God without hope who controls others or punishes eternally. A hopeful God never stops loving, seeking to convince everyone to say, "yes!" to love.[18]

LIFE-CHANGING

The phrase "life-changing" appears in this book's subtitle: "An Introduction to Life-Changing Ideas." Over the years, I've discovered that open and relational ideas alter — for good — how people think and act. I've stopped keeping track of how many have told me this perspective changed their lives.

To close, though, I want to share a few more stories. I've simplified each and, in most in cases, changed the names of the storytellers. Some people get booted out of families and communities or lose their jobs for embracing open and relational ideas. I hope changing their names can provide protection and privacy.

Michele sends me audio messages on Facebook Messenger. In nearly every message, she thanks me for introducing her to open and relational theology. She has extensive formal training under conventional theologians like R. C. Sproul, but Michele found their theology stifling, harmful, and... sexist. In a recent voice message, she said, "Isn't it odd that they would take tuition money from me, a woman, despite thinking I should never be allowed to teach!"

James is a retired physicist who often felt uneasy with conventional ideas about God. But the scientism he encountered among some in his profession also made him uneasy, because science cannot provide all truths. Open and relational theology gave him a framework into which he could place his experiences of beauty, love, and purpose alongside his work in physics. "I only wish I'd discovered this theology earlier," he told me recently.

One of my doctoral students came to open and relational theology wanting to make sense of his changing views of sexuality. He believed in God but could not embrace theologies that portrayed all humans as black-and-white binaries rather than multi-dimensional, as static rather than fluid. "Starting with a loving and uncontrolling God," he said, "opens up possibilities for me to make sense of sex and gender."

Jone was a famous Evangelical who traveled the world sharing her faith. But questions about suffering—her own and others—led Jone out of evangelicalism. "I don't know if I'll ever believe in God again," she said recently. "But if I do, it will be an open and relational God." I can't help but think she is, as Jesus would say, "not far from the kingdom of God."

Maliq grew up with a Muslim mother and Catholic father. He sometimes calls himself "nonreligious," "multireligious," and once, "a God-mutt." Open and relational concepts help him sort through what's positive in various traditions without requiring him to say any had the full truth. He represents a growing number of people who believe in God but don't "fit" traditional religious categories.

Similarly, Andrew embraced open and relational theology because it helps him makes sense of religious diversity. "If God is present to everyone and reveals in an uncontrolling way," he said to me, "we should expect a variety of religions and diverse views of God." This doesn't mean any religion is as good as another. Nor is any view of God as true as another. But open and relational thought provides a conceptual basis to validate the variety of religious expressions and provide reasons to think some beliefs are more plausible than others.

I met Lori while hiking and photographing in the California wilderness. "Nature is my church," she said as we talked on a Yosemite National Park bus. Subsequent email discussions led her to believe in a wild, open, and relational God. "Don't ask me to put a foot in a man-made cathedral," she wrote, "but I believe in the God of John Muir, and He builds beautiful cathedrals in nature!"

Barry is an activist who says the open and relational vision helps him work for social justice and promote personal responsibility. The open and relational God doesn't singlehandedly set one group in authority or by decree establish the status quo. So much of our current situation needs changing. Barry believes the common good depends, in part, on joining with God to help the discriminated against and hurting. We each have a personal responsibility in the work of love.

Just last week, I talked with Kathy about the purpose of life. At one point, she asked, "So... what should I do with myself?" She wanted an answer big enough to orient the day-by-day choices she makes. "An open and relational vision might say your purpose is to love," I said, "but what love looks like in each moment takes a myriad of forms." In her work as a schoolteacher, her artistic interests, and family relationships, Kathy can join God in loving the world into a better existence.

I've stopped keeping a record of how many people say they couldn't believe in God if it were not for open and relational theology. Many thought they had to choose between atheism and the conventional God. Some who discover open and relational theology remain in historic faith communities. Others choose not to. Some were never part of a tradition and send notes asking me to connect them to like-minded people. Many have gone through a painful process of deconstructing theological beliefs and only recently discovered open and relational thought. They feel as though they've "come home," because the ideas make so much sense.

My point: lives are changing.

By now, you probably understand why open and relational theology appeals to me and many others.

This way of thinking helps us orient our lives and understand reality. It helps us love our partners and those who harm us, our friends and strangers, other creatures and God. It's rational and livable, fits both head and heart.

It's a way of wisdom.

I began this book with these words: "People across the globe are discovering open and relational theology." This book is more than a description of open and relational theology to help you discover it too, although that's its primary purpose. It's also an invitation:

I invite you to embrace an open, relational, and loving God.

QUESTIONS:

1. Before you read this book, how did you understand the meaning of *agape*?
2. Which advantages of love in open and relational theology do you find most attractive?
3. What's the difference between thinking we desire God and saying we love God by affecting God's well-being?
4. Do you think it's possible to have a personal relationship with a loving God? Explain how this view might be meaningful, attractive, or problematic.
5. How does Jesus teach or illustrate an open and relational perspective?
6. How might the open and relational view of God be relevant to your life?

Scan the QR code for a video lecture on love's essential aspects and diverse forms - Center for Christian Thought.

APPENDIX

WHO IS OPEN AND RELATIONAL?

For several decades, I've opted to identify a few basic ideas that comprise the umbrella I call "open and relational theology."[1] Under that umbrella stand many people, movements, and claims. I've described the basic ideas of this theology in this book.

Open and relational thinkers believe God gives and receives in relation to creation. That's relational. Both God and creatures experientially move into an open future. That's open. I've also talked about God's love and presence in the universe. And so on.

Open and relational thinkers don't agree on everything. My emphasis on a big umbrella doesn't mean those differences are inconsequential. Difference matters. There's always a place for exploring and noting them. Exploring differences is part of the fun of living in relationship with God and others—at least when it's done respectfully!

I invite readers to explore this rich diversity by consulting the authors and books I list at the conclusion of this book.

Many people ask me to differentiate between process, open, and relational theologies. They want to know, for instance, what makes process theology different from open theology. Some ask about the differences between open theology and relational thought. And some wonder if all relational theologies are process theologies (they aren't).

These are good questions. Answering each well requires identifying the essential ideas of each theology. A close look at those who self-identify as process, openness, or relational reveals diverse lists of essentials. What is essential to one person's theological view is not to another. And there's no official list.

It's easier if we look at the ideas proposed by specific people. I can point to differences and similarities between Catherine Keller and Gregory Boyd, for instance, but even that evaluating can get complicated.

I sometimes respond to these questions by saying, "the typical, self-identifying open theist believes x." Or "the typical, self-identifying process theist believes y." These generalizations help, but they don't account for many who don't fit what's "typical." Some self-identify with one label, say "process theology," but hold views typical of another label, say "open theology." Confusion reigns.

Instead of building a massive chart, constructing a thematic tree with roots and branches, or making a list of "10 Essential Ideas of _ _ _ Theology," I point to two general views as common for open and relational thinkers: God is relational, and the future is open. I then celebrate, ponder, and argue over the diverse ways to understand these ideas and others.

I admit this "big tent" approach is sometimes messy. But I find it more effective than either a strict list of beliefs or a "whatever works for you" approach. The first excludes all but a select few who affirm every jot and tittle. The second promotes confusion and renders labels meaningless. The big tent approach is broadly inclusive without dismissing distinctions.

Open and relational thinkers come from or identify with various religions and movements. I've done no official survey, but I'm confident more open and relational thinkers identify with Christianity than any other religion. The Christian denominations and movements with which open and relational thinkers identify are diverse.

You can find open and relational Adventists, African Methodist Episcopal, Anglicans, Baptists, Church of Christ, Church of England, Church of God, Church of the Nazarene, Congregationalists, Covenant, Disciples of Christ, Eastern Orthodox, Episcopal, Free Methodists, Latter-Day Saints, Lutherans, Mennonites, Methodists, Pentecostals, Presbyterians, Quakers, Roman Catholics, Salvation Army, Unitarians, United/ Uniting Churches, United Church of Christ, and more.

Open and relational thinkers sometimes identify primarily with a particular way of thinking rather than with a specific denomination or religion. There are open and relational Anabaptists, analytic theologians, Arminians, Calvinists, charismatics, continentalists, evangelicals, exvangelicals, feminists, intersectionalists, liberationists, postcolonialists, progressives, theopoetics, Wesleyan, and womanists.

Some open and relational thinkers are members of other religious and non-religious traditions. Those include African religions, Bahai, Buddhism, Indigenous religions, Interfaith, Islam, Judaism, Nones, Paganism, Spiritual but not Religious, and more.

I see this diversity as a strength. The ideas of open and relational theology transcend any one group or religion. The movement is broad enough and ideas appealing enough to appreciate the diversity, while pointing to a few ideas that unite.

By the way, I'm always interested in adding to the above list of religions, Christian denominations, or other labels open and relational thinkers embrace. Send me a note if I've missed a label on my list.

ABOUT THE AUTHOR

Thomas Jay Oord, Ph.D., is a theologian, philosopher, and scholar of multi-disciplinary studies. He directs doctoral students at Northwind Theological Seminary and the Center for Open and Relational Theology. Oord is an award-winning author and has written or edited more than twenty-five books. A gifted speaker, Oord lectures at universities, conferences, churches, and institutions around the globe. He is known for contributions to research on love, science and religion, open and relational theology, the problem of suffering, and the implications of freedom for transformational relationships.

For information on Northwind Theological Seminary's doctoral program in Open and Relational Theology, which follows the Oxford learning style and is fully online, see... **northwindseminary. org/center-for-open-relational-theology**

For information on the Center for Open and Relational Theology, see... **c4ort.com**

For the author's website, see... **thomasjayoord.com**

GOING DEEPER

Key Open and Relational Books (Written Since 1990) and Authors...

To go deeper on **artificial intelligence**, see...
Ilia Delio, *Reechanting the Earth: Why AI Needs Religion* (Orbis, 2020).
And other books on the subject by Micah Redding.

To go deeper on **atonement**, see...
Andrew Sung Park, *Triune Atonement* (John Knox, 2009).
Larry Shelton, *Cross and Covenant* (Paternoster, 2006).

And other books by Paul Fiddes, Rodger Rushing, and Marit Trelstad.

To go deeper on **beauty, theopoetics, and aesthetics**, see...
Patricia Adams Farmer, *Embracing a Beautiful God* (2013).

And other books on the subject by Katelynn Carver, Daniel
Dombrowski, Roland Faber, Jon Gill, Patricia Adams Farmer, Callid
Keefe-Perry, Catherine Keller, Jay McDaniel, and Keith Ward.

To go deeper on **biblical studies**, see...
Gregory Boyd, *Inspired Imperfection* (Fortress, 2020).
Ronald Farmer, *Process Theology and Biblical Interpretation* (Energion,
2021).
Terence Fretheim, *God and World in the Old Testament* (Abingdon, 2005).
Gabriel Gordon, *God Speaks* (Quoir, 2021).
Russell Preagant, *Reading the Bible for All the Wrong Reasons*
(Fortress, 2011).

And other books on the subject by William Beardslee, Walter
Brueggeman, Robert Cornwall, Troy Edwards, Ronald Farmer,

Christopher Fisher, Michael Lodahl, Richard Middleton, TC Moore, Nick Page, Russell Pregeant, Manuel Schmid, Eric Siebert, Scott Spencer, Ekaputra Tupamahu, Michael Widmer, Karen Winslow, and William Yarchin.

To go deeper on **church and ecclesiology**, see
Philip Clayton, *Transforming Christian Theology* (Fortress, 2009).
Bruce Epperly, *Church Ahead* (Energion, 2020).
Marjorie Suchocki, *God-Christ-Church* (Herder and Herder, 1992).

And other books on the subject by Robert Cornwall, Thomas Hermans-Webster, Sheri Kling, Sheryl Kujawa-Holbrook, Libby Tedder Hugus, Sarah Heaner Lancaster, Brian McLaren, Mary Elizabeth Moore, Timothy Murphy, Daniel Ott, John Reader, and Casey Sigmon.

To go deeper on **creation, science, and theology**, see…
Ian Barbour, *Nature, Human Nature, and God* (Fortress, 2002).
Ilia Delio, *The Emergent Christ* (Orbis, 2011).
John Polkinghorne, *The Polkinghorne Reader* (Templeton, 2009).

And other books on the subject by Ian Barbour, Rick Barr, Joseph Bracken, John Buchanan, Anna Case-Winters, Philip Clayton, Robin Collins, Peter Colyer, Rem Edwards, Michael Epperson, John Haught, Gary Herstein, Matthew Hill, Nancy Howell, John Jungerman, Catherine Keller, Jeffrey Koperski, Jerry Korsmeyer, Michael Lodahl, Bradford McCall, Manuel David Morales, David Nikkel, Thomas Jay Oord, John Polkinghorne, Andre Rabe, Tim Reddish, Joshua Reichard, Anne Runehov, Matthew Segall, Keith Ward, Janet Warren, and Josef Zycinski.

To go deeper on **deconstructing** traditional theology, see…
Brian McLaren, *Faith After Doubt* (St. Martins, 2021).
Mark Karris, *Religious Refugees* (Quoir, 2020).

And see books on the subject by David Ray Griffin and Catherine Keller.

To go deeper on **ecology**, see…
Philip Clayton and Wm Andrew Schwartz, *What is Ecological Civilization?* (Process Century, 2019).
Jay McDaniel, *With Roots and Wings* (Wipf and Stock, 2009).
Sallie McFague, *Life Abundant* (Fortress, 2001).
Randy Woodley, *Shalom and the Community of Creation* (Eerdmans, 2012).

And other books on the subject by Ignacio Castuera, John Cobb, John Culp, Ilia Delio, Jacob Erickson, Sharon Harvey, Krista Hughes, Carol Johnston, Catherine Keller, and Michael Lodahl.

To go deeper on **eschatology** and **hope**, see
Joseph Bracken, *World Without End* (Eerdmans, 2005).
Catherine Keller, *Facing Apocalypse* (Orbis, 2021).
John Polkinghorne, *The God of Hope and the End of the World* (Yale, 2002).

And other books on the subject by Sharon Baker Putt, Bradley Jersak, Catherine Keller, Juergen Moltmann, John Polkingorne, Marjorie Suchocki, Keith Ward, and Keith Yandell.

To go deeper on **evil**, see...
David Ray Griffin, *God Exists but Gawd Does Not* (Process Century, 2011).
Thomas Jay Oord, *God Can't* (SacraSage, 2019).
William Paul Young, *The Shack* (Windblown, 2007).

And see books on the subject by Anna Case-Winters, David Ray Griffin, William Hasker, Tyron Inbody, Janyne McConnaughey, Keith Putt, Tim Reddish, Joshua Reichard, Richard Rice, Bethany Sollereder, and Marjorie Suchocki.

To go deeper on **feminism**, see...
Monica Coleman, Nancy Howell, and Helene Russell, eds., *Creating Women's Theology* (Pickwick, 2011).
Karen Winslow, *Imagining Equity* (Wesley's Foundery, 2021).

And see books on the subject by Monica Coleman, Nancy Howell, Sarah Heaner Lancaster, Catherine Keller, and Marjorie Suchocki.

To go deeper on **freedom**, see...
Jeffrey F. Keuss, *Freedom of the Self* (Pickwick, 2010).
Timothy O'Connor, *Persons and Causes* (Oxford, 2002).

And see books by David Basinger, Delwin Brown, and Simon Kittle.

To go deeper on **God's emotions**, see...
Juergen Moltmann, *The Crucified God* (Fortress, 2015).
Terryl and Fiona Givens, *The God Who Weeps* (Deseret, 2017).

And other books on the subject by RT Mullins.

To go deeper on **God's knowledge**, see...
Clark Pinnock, et. al., *The Openness of God* (IVP, 2004).
Richard Rice, *God's Foreknowledge and Man's Free Will* (Wipf and Stock, 2004).
Michael Saia, *Does God Know the Future?* (Xulon, 2014).

And other books on the subject by James Goetz, William Hasker, Winkey Pratney, and Alan Rhoda.

To go deeper on **God's power**, see...
Anna Case-Winters, *God's Power* (Westminster/John Knox, 1990).
Thomas Jay Oord, *The Uncontrolling Love of God* (IVP, 2015).

And other books by David Basinger, Jason Clark, Sheila Greeve Davaney, Julia Enxing, and David Ray Griffin.

To go deeper on **God's relationality** and **suffering**, see...
Terrence Fretheim, *The Suffering of God* (Fortress, 1984).
Jurgen Moltmann, *The Crucified God* (Fortress, 2015).
Roberto Sirvent, *Embracing Vulnerability* (Pickwick, 2014).

And other books by Paul Fiddes, Jeff Pool, Brent Schmidt, and Scott Spencer.

To go deeper on the **Holy Spirit**, see...
Clark H. Pinnock, *Flame of Love* (IVP, 1999).

And other books by Michael Lodahl and Blair Reynolds.

To go deeper on **Jesus** and **Christology**, see...
Gregory Boyd, *Cross Vision* (Fortress, 2018).
John B. Cobb, Jr., *Jesus' Abba* (Fortress, 2016).
Tripp Fuller, *Jesus: Liar, Lunatic, Lord, or Awesome?* (Fortress, 2015).
Brad Jersak, *A More Christlike God* (Plain Truth, 2016).
Richard Rohr, *The Universal Christ* (Convergent, 2021).

And other books on the subject by Allan Bevere, Donna Bowman, Gregory Boyd, Rita Nakashima Brock, Barry Callen, Rebecca Copeland, Tripp Fuller, Tyron Inbody, Dyton Owen, Sharon Baker Putt, Rodger Rushing, Scott Spencer, Marit Trelstad, and Kurt Willems.

To go deeper on **Judaism**, see...
Bradley Shavit Artson, *Renewing the Process of Creation* (Jewish Lights, 2016).
Shai Held, *Abraham Joshua Heschel* (Indiana University, 2013).

And see books on the subject by Harold Kushner and Sandra Lubarsky.

To go deeper on **leadership**, see...
Roland Hearn, Sheri D. Kling, and Thomas Jay Oord, eds., *Open and Relational Leadership* (SacraSage 2020).

To go deeper on **love**, see...
Thomas Jay Oord, *The Nature of Love* (Chalice, 2010).
David Polk, *God of Empowering Love* (Process Century, 2016)
Paul Sponheim, *Love's Availing Power* (Fortress, 2011).

And see books on the subject by Craig A. Boyd, Jared Byas, Barry Callen, Gary Chartier, Jason Clark, Rem Edwards, Franklin Gamwell, Paul Joseph Greene, Kurian Kachappilly, L Michaels, Elaine Padilla, David Polk, and Johan Tredoux.

To go deeper on **mental illness**, see...
Monica Coleman, *Bipolar Faith* (Fortress, 2016).

And see books on the subject by Greg Denniston.

To go deeper on **missions and missional theology**, see...
Vaughn Baker, *Evangelism and the Openness of God* (Wipf and Stock, 2012).
Clark Pinnock, *A Wideness in God's Mercy* (Zondervan, 1992).

And other books on the subject by John Sanders and Peter C. Wagner.

To go deeper on **Native American spirituality**, see...
Randy Woodley, *Shalom and the Community of Creation* (Eerdmans, 2012).

To go deeper on **nonviolence**, see...
Sharon Baker Putt, *A Nonviolent Theology of Love* (Fortress, 2021).
Eric Seibert, *The Violence of Scripture* (Fortress, 2012).

And see books by Jonathan Foster.

To explore overviews of **open theology**, see...
Gregory Boyd, *God of the Possible* (Baker, 2000).
Clark Pinnock, et. al., *The Openness of God* (IVP, 1994).
Richard Rice, *The Future of Open Theism* (IVP, 2020).

And see books on the subject by the authors above and William Hasker, John Sanders, Manuel Schmid, and Larry Witham.

To go deeper on **panentheism**, see...
Andrew Davis and Philip Clayton, *How I Found God in Everyone and Everywhere* (Monkfish, 2018).
Philip Clayton and Arthur Peacocke, *In Whom We Live and Move and Have Our Being* (Eerdmans, 2004).

And see books on the subject by Godehard Bruntrup, John Culp, and David Ray Griffin.

To go deeper on **philosophical theology**, see
Philip Clayton, *The Problem of God in Modern Thought* (Eerdmans, 2000).
Roland Faber, *God as the Poet of the World* (Westminster/John Knox, 2004).

David Ray Griffin, *Reenchantment without Supernaturalism* (Cornell, 2000).

Richard Swinburne, *The Coherence of Theism* (Oxford, 1993).

And see books on the subject by Randall Auxier, David Basinger, Joseph Bracken, Rufus Burrow, Jr., Carol Christ, Mark Davies, Andrew Davis, Daniel Dombrowski, Rem Edwards, Julia Enxing, Peter Forrest, Lewis Ford, Derek Malone-France, Stephen Franklin, James Goetz, Johannes Groessl, William Hasker, Brittney Hartley, Curtis Holtzen, J.R. Hustwit, Darren Iammarino, Catherine Keller, Simon Kittle, Jeffrey Koperski, Brian Macallan, James McLachlan, Robert Mesle, Ryan Mullins, Robert Neville, David Nikkel, Thomas Jay Oord, Elaine Padilla, B. Keith Putt, Joshua Rasmussen, John Reader, Matthew Segall, Farhan Shah, Aaron Simons, Atle Ottesen Sovik, Donald Viney, Theodore Walker, Keith Ward, Michel Weber, Demian Wheeler, David Woodruff, and Dean Zimmerman.

To go deeper on **politics and social issues**, see...
Greg Boyd, *The Myth of a Christian Nation* (Zondervan, 2005).
Bruce Epperly, *Process Theology and Politics* (Energion, 2020).
Catherine Keller, *Facing Apocalypse* (Orbis, 2021).

And see books on the subject by David Ray Griffin, Justin Heinzekehr, and Randall C. Morris.

To go deeper on **prayer**, see...
Bruce Epperly, *Praying with Process Theology* (River Lane, 2017).
Mark Karris, *Divine Echoes* (Quoir, 2018)
Marjorie Suchocki, *In God's Presence* (Chalice, 1996).

And see books on the subject by Vincent Brummer, Thomas Jay Oord, and Michael Saia.

To explore **process theology** overviews, see
Bradley Shavit Artson, *God of Becoming and Relationship* (Jewish Lights, 2016).
Bruce Epperly, *Process Theology* (T&T Clark, 2011).
Catherine Keller, *On the Mystery* (Fortress, 2007).
Robert Mesle, *Process Theology* (Chalice, 1993).

And see books on the subject by Donna Bowman, Joseph Bracken, John B. Cobb, Jr., Roland Faber, David Ray Griffin, Catherine Keller, Jay McDaniel, Robert Mesle, and Marjorie Suchocki,

To go deeper on **providence**, see...
Thomas Jay Oord, *The Uncontrolling Love of God* (IVP, 2015).
John Sanders, *The God Who Risks* (IVP, 2007).

And see material on the website bibliography from David
Bartholomew, Rob Fringer and Jeff Lane, Curtis Holtzen, John
Polkinghorne, Keith Ward, and Michael Zbaraschuk.

To explore **relational theology**, see
Terence Fretheim, *God So Enters Relationships That* (Fortress, 2020).
Curtis Holtzen, *The God Who Trusts* (IVP, 2019).
Brint Montgomery, Thomas Jay Oord, and Karen Winslow, eds.,
Relational Theology (Point Loma, 2012).

And see books on the subject from James Loder, Michael Lodahl, and
Thomas Jay Oord.

To go deeper on **religious pluralism**, see
Jay McDaniel, *Ghandi's Hope* (Orbis, 2005).
David Ray Griffin, *Deep Religious Pluralism* (John Knox, 2005).
Marjorie Suchocki, *Divinity and Diversity* (Abingdon, 2003).

And see books on the subject by Tim Burnette, John B. Cobb, Jr.,
Roland Faber, David Ray Griffin, JR Hustwit, Brian McLaren, Andrew
Schwartz, John Paul Sydnor, John Thatamanil, and Keith Ward.

To explore **salvation**, see
John Cobb, *Salvation: Jesus' Mission and Ours* (Process Century,
2020).
John Sanders, *Embracing Prodigals* (Wipf and Stock, 2020).

And see books on the subject by Sharon Baker Putt and Keith Ward.

To go deeper on **sexuality and marriage**, see...
Kathlyn A. Breazeale, *Mutual Empowerment* (Fortress, 2008).

And see books by Michael Brennan, Jacob Erickson, and Jonathan
Foster.

To go deeper on **sin**, see...
Andrew Sung Park, *The Wounded Heart of God* (Abingdon, 1994).
Marjorie Suchocki, *The Fall to Violence* (Continuum, 1995).

To go deeper on **spirituality and spiritual formation**, see...
John B. Cobb, Jr., *Salvation* (Process Century 2020)
Bruce Epperly, *Holy Adventure* (Upper Room, 2008).
Patricia Farmer, *Embracing a Beautiful God* (Chalice, 2003).
Sheri D. Kling, *A Process Spirituality* (Lexington, 2020).
Brian McLaren, *We Make the Road by Walking* (Jericho, 2015).

And see books on the subject by Rob Bell, Barry Callen, Katelynn
Carver, John Cobb and Clark Pinnock, Bruce Epperly, David Ray

Griffin, Daniel Held, Jason Jones, Pamela Ebstyne King, Sarah Heaner Lancaster, David Matthew, Jay McDaniel, L Michaels, Richard Rohr, Michael Rose, and Nora Speakman.

To go deeper on **spiritual warfare**, see...
Greg Boyd, *Satan and the Problem of Evil* (IVP, 2001).

To go deeper on **theological education**, see...
Mary Elizabeth Moore, *Teaching from the Heart* (Fortress, 1991).

And see books by Thomas Estes, Sheryl Kujawa-Holbrook, Bonnie Rambob, and John Reader.

To go deeper on **time**, see...
Ryan Mullins, *The End of a Timeless God* (Oxford, 2016).

And see books on the subject by Robert Adams, Jeffrey Koperski, Alan Padgett, George Shields, Donald Viney, Nicholas Wolterstorff, and Dean Zimmerman

To go deeper on **trauma and healing**, see...
Janyne McConnaughey, *Brave* (Cladach, 2015)
Andrew Sung Park, *From Hurt to Healing* (Abingdon, 2004).

And see books on the subject by Barry Callen and Ryan Lambros.

To go deeper on **trinity**, see...
Karen Baker-Fletcher, *Dancing with God* (Chalice, 2006).
Joseph Bracken: *God: Three Who Are One* (Liturgical, 2017).
Dale Tuggy, *What is the Trinity?* (Createspace, 2017).
Keith Ward, *Christ and Cosmos* (Cambridge, 2015).

And see books on the subject by Karen Baker-Fletcher, Gregory Boyd, Joseph A. Bracken, Lewis Ford, William Hasker, Lynne Lorenzen, Juergen Moltmann, Steven Studebaker, Marjorie Hewitt Suchocki, Dale Tuggy, and Keith Ward

To go deeper on **Wesleyanism, John Wesley, Methodism**, see...
John B. Cobb, Jr. *Grace and Responsibility* (Abingdon, 1995).
Bryan P. Stone and Thomas Jay Oord, eds., *Thy Nature and Name is Love* (Kingswood, 2001).

And see books on the subject by John B. Cobb, Jr., John Culp, Rem Edwards, Matt Hill, Michael Lodahl, Maynard Moore, Hilde Marie Øgreid Movafagh, Thomas Jay Oord, Rory Randall, Andrew Schwartz, and Marjorie Suchocki.

To go deeper on **womanist theology**, see

Karen Baker-Fletcher, *Dancing with God* (Chalice, 2006).

Monica Coleman, *Making a Way Out of No Way* (Fortress, 2008).

This list will be expanded. What or who should be added? Contact the author with your suggestions.

**NORTHWIND SEMINARY'S
ONLINE DOCTORAL PROGRAM
IN OPEN & RELATIONAL THEOLOGY**

Those interested in pursuing a doctoral degree in open and relational theology should contact Thomas Jay Oord. The program he directs at Northwind Theological Seminary follows the Oxford University method, which means students work directly with Dr. Oord. The program is fully online, which means students need not relocate. For more information, see the Northwind Theological Seminary website or contact Dr. Oord.

Scan the QR code for a video discussion of the Open and Relational Theology doctoral program.

ACKNOWLEDGEMENTS

I've been thinking lately about how indebted I am. How indebted we *all* are. No words of gratitude or gestures of appreciation will account for all the ways I've been helped. I could never acknowledge everyone.

Especially difficult to acknowledge are the thinkers, teachers, and sages who have been pondering and promulgating the ideas I describe in this book. Some are religious people, others are philosophers, some scientists, artists, and more. The wisdom of everyday people without official titles has also influenced me profoundly.

Below is a list of people who read the early manuscript, made suggestions, or promoted the book. I *really* appreciate their help. Those people include Rebecca Adams, Josh Andrews, Maria Arroyave, Jez Bayes, John Beresford, Michael Brennan, Jared Byas, Dan Cathey, Harry Chou, John Coats, John Cobb, Gloria Coffin, Tamara Coleman, Sarey Martin Concepcion, John Culp, Adam D'Achille, John Dally, Ulrick Dam, Paul Dazet, Pete Enns, Brian Felushko, Tripp Fuller, Gabriel Gordon, Matt Hill, Todd Holden, Stacy Holmes, Greg Hoover, Eric Hughes, Libby and

Jeremy Hugus, Patti Laushman, Bob Keay, Travis Keller, Shaleen Kendrick, Dan Kent, Lori Kitchen, Dan Koch, John Loppnow, Jeff Lowe, Phil Mazzeo, Janyne McConnaughey, L Michaels, Tim Miller, Paul Morris, Ryan T. Mullins, Alexa Oord, Josh Patterson, Seth Price, Andre Rabe, Mary-Anne Rabe, Charles Revis, Cindy Riddell, Michael Rose, Shane Russo, Shawn Ryan, Lemuel Sandoval, JC Sheridan, Neil Short, Carolyn Joy Simpson, Jon Steingard, Jeffrey Timmons, Ian Todd, Mark Umstot, Todd Vick, Tim Victor, Steve Watson, Bethanie Young, Deanna Young,

This book is dedicated to God... in part, because the God I believe in delights even in book dedications!

ENDNOTES

1. WHY

1. Paul Froese and Christopher Bader, *America's Four Gods: What We Say About God — and What That Says About Us* (Oxford: Oxford University Press, 2010) 4, 149.

2. To my knowledge, it remains largely unstudied how people in other countries think about God — at least in terms of these categories. I suspect there are surprising similarities and interesting differences.

3. The percentages: Authoritative (32%), Benevolent (24%), Distant (24%), and Critical (16%). See chapter one in See chapter one in *America's Four Gods*.

4. Ibid., 28-29.

5. For deeper exploration of how views of God correspond with values and orientations in life, see John Sanders, *Embracing Prodigals: Overcoming Authoritative Religion by Embodying Jesus' Nurturing Grace* (Eugene, OR: Cascade, 2020). Sanders cites psychological and sociological studies in his book.

6. Froese and Bader, *America's Four Gods*, 15.

7. Ibid., 35.

8. Ibid., 32.

9. On this, see John Sanders, *Embracing Prodigals*.

10. Exod 34:6-7; etc.

11. *Qu'ran* 1:1-3.

12. 1 Jn 4:8,16.

13. Note to fellow Christians with a high view of the Bible: I could have written this book and profusely peppered it with biblical passages. I think the Bible strongly supports an open and relational view, although I admit some passages have been interpreted in ways that fit conventional theology. I chose not to cite the Bible frequently (although I do occassionally), because I want to appeal to those without much knowledge of scripture. I also write to those burnt-out or even abused by those who, often with good intentions, have used the Bible more as a weapon than as medicine. To go deeper on the ways the Bible supports an open and relational perspective, consult the books and authors I mention in the "Going Deeper" section of this book.

14. Heb. 1:3.

15. 1 John 3:16.

2. OPEN

1. One alternative to open and relational theology goes by the name "middle knowledge" or "Molinism." It says God chose to create this world among the possible worlds God could have created. When choosing, God looked at how all worlds would play out. God can look into the future, says Molinism, and foresee every future decision.

Debates on middle knowledge are technical, and this book is not the place to explore the details, such as the status of counterfactuals and the grounding problem. But we don't need the details to see a problem with middle knowledge. Our story about Andee and ice cream illustrates it.

The middle knowledge view says God can foreknow with certainty that Andee gets chocolate. If a mistake-free God foreknows Andee gets chocolate, Andee *must* get chocolate. God can't make a mistake, so Andee's not free to do otherwise. From the perspective of open and relational theologians (and others), Molinism is incoherent. There's never a time (even before God created our world) the outcomes of free decisions can be known in advance.

2. Carl F. H. Henry, *God, Revelation, and Authority: The God who Stands and Stays,* Part One, vol. 5. (Waco: Word 1982), 304.

3. Augustine, *The Trinity* V. 5. (New York: New City Press, 2012).

4. James 1:17.

5. Malachi 3:7.

6. Many process-oriented theists prefer the dipolar theism label. Charles Hartshorne raised the label to prominence. See his essay "The Dipolar Conception of Deity," *Review of Metaphysics* 21:2 (1967), 273-89) and Donald Viney. "Hartshorne's Dipolar Theism and the Mystery of God" *Philosophia*, 35 (2007), 341-350.

7. After Charles Darwin, it has become less common to think creatures have essences or natures. So, this analogy isn't perfect. But Darwin's views don't affect the idea that God has an unchanging essence. In fact, God may be the only being with an essence.

8. Lamentations 3:22.

9. Lamentations 3:23.

10. For an example of how prayer opens up new opportunities, see my prayers for a Covid-19 patient in chapter two of my book *Questions and Answers for God Can't* (SacraSage, 2020).

3. RELATIONAL

1. Thomas Aquinas, *Summa Theologica*, I (Westminster, Md: Christian Classics, 1981), q. 6, a.2, ad 1.

2. Thomas Aquinas, *Summa Contra Gentiles* II (Notre Dame, Ind.: University of Notre Dame Press, 1981), 13-14.

3. Maimonides, *A Guide for the Perplexed,* rev. ed. (Dover, 2000), Chapter 11.

4. See Thomas Jay Oord *God Can't: How to Believe in God and Love after Tragedy, Abuse, and Other Evils* (SacraSage, 2019), chapter 2.

5. Genesis 1:26.

6. See the resources page at the conclusion of this book for more info on these thinkers.

7. See the resources page at the conclusion of this book for more info on these thinkers.

4. AMIPOTENT

1. For a concise exploration of this, see Alfred R. Mele, *Free: Why Science Hasn't Disproved Free Will* (Oxford, 2014).

2. John Polkinghorne, *Belief in God in an Age of Science* (Yale, 1998).

3. See my books *God Can't: How to Believe in God and Love after Tragedy, Abuse, and Other Evils* (SacraSage 2019) and *The Uncontrolling Love of God* (IVP Academic, 2015).

4. For open and relational essays on partnering with God, see Timothy Reddish, Bonnie Rambob, Fran Stedman, and Thomas Jay Oord, eds. *Partnering with God: Exploring Collaboration in Open and Relational Theology* (SacraSage, 2021).

5. Oord, *God Can't.*

6. Alfred North Whitehead, *Process and Reality: An Essay in Cosmology* David Ray Griffin and Donald Sherburne, eds., (Free Press, 1978), 351.

7. Oord, *Questions and Answers for God Can't.*

5. PRESENT

1. To see the way various open and relational theologians think about creation from nothing, see Thomas Jay Oord, ed., *Theologies of Creation: Creatio ex Nihilo and Its New Rivals* (Routledge, 2014).

2. Ian Barbour, *Religion in an Age of Science* (Harper One, 1997).

3. Find a helpful discussion of panentheism in John Culp's entry, https://plato.stanford.edu/entries/panentheism/

4. Find this list in Philip Clayton and Arthur Peacocke, *In Whom We Live and Move and Have Our Being* (Eerdmans, 2004).

5. For more on my view of panexperientialism/panpsychism, see Thomas Jay Oord and Wm. Andrew Schwartz, "Panentheism and Panexperientialism for Open and Relational Theology," in *Panentheism and Panpsychism: Philosophy of Religion Meets Philosophy of Mind*, Godehard Brüntrup, et. al., eds., (Mentis Verlag/Brill, 2020).

6. Philippians 2:12

7. Philippians 2:13

8. I Cor. 3:7.

9. See Thomas Jay Oord, *Questions and Answers for God Can't*, ch. 7.

6. LOVING

1. Anders Nygren, *Agape and Eros*, tr. Philip S. Watson (New York: Harper and Row, 1957 [1930]).

2. Augustine, *Teaching Christianity* (De Doctrina Christiana), ed. John E. Rotelle, O.S.A, trans. Edmund Hill, O.P. (Hyde Park, N.Y.: New City Press, 1996).

3. I devote a chapter to Augustine's view of love and its problems in my book *The Nature of Love* (Chalice, 2010), ch. 3.

4. For details on these problems, see *The Nature of Love*, chs. 2–3.

5. In addition to *The Nature of Love* and *The Uncontrolling Love of God,* see my books *Defining Love* (Brazos, 2010) and *The Science of Love* (Templeton, 2004).

6. Jay McDaniel emphasizes the idea that love involves listening. See https://www.openhorizons.org/the-listening-side-of-love.html

7. John B. Cobb, Jr. And David Ray Griffin, *Process Theology: An Introductory Exposition* (Louisville, KY: Westminster/John Knox, 1976).

8. See Ephesians 5:1.

9. In various writings, I've explained how in one sense, God must love, and in another sense, God freely chooses to love. God's nature is love, and God cannot do otherwise than love. But because the future is open and God can't foreknow what will occur, God freely chooses how to love in each moment, not certain which of the loving options would be most effective when creatures later respond. For more, see my books *The Uncontrolling Love of God*, ch. 7 and *Questions and Answers for God Can't*, ch. 4.

10. Romans 8:38-39

11. Galatians 5:6

12. Matthew 22:35-40; 1 Corinthians 13:13; 1 John 4:8, 16.

13. See Bryan P. Stone and Thomas Jay Oord, eds., *Thy Nature and Thy Name is Love: Process and Wesleyan Theologies in Dialogue* (Kingswood, 2001).

14. See my discussion of Augustine's love theology in *The Nature of Love*, ch. 3.

15. Ibid.

16. I have explained this definition of love in numerous publications. See especially, *Defining Love*, chs. 1-2.

17. 1 Corinthians 13:5, 7.

18. For more about a God who hopes (and trusts), see Curtis Holtzen, *The God Who Trusts* (IVP Academic, 2019).

APPENDIX: WHO IS OPEN AND RELATIONAL?

1. I coined the label "Open and Relational Theology" to bring together isolated groups and individuals who share basic views about God's relation to time, divine relation to creatures, creaturely freedom, an emphasis upon love, and more. The impetus for coining the label was my applying to form this group at the American Academy of Religion, joined by my co-chair Lynne Lorenzen. The group remains a strong voice at AAR, and as of this writing is co-chaired by Krista Hughes and Andrew Schwartz.

INDEX

aesthetics / art / beauty 15, 86-88, 93-94, 98-99, 153

afterlife 3-4, 13, 20-21, 91, 104, 111-113, 118, 125, 140

agape 119-121

agnostic 6, 12, 14

Allah 20, 31

annihilation 13, 112-113, 125

anthropomorphism 54

apophaticism 55

atheism 14, 56, 84, 130-131, 136, 140, 143

atonement 17, 103-106, 153

attunement 105-106

Augustine 38, 120-122, 133-134

Baker-Fletcher, Karen 62

Barbour, Ian 95

Beach Boys 5

Bible / scripture x, 7, 11, 15, 21, 30-31, 38-39, 41, 44-45, 50-52, 63-64,
81, 105, 117, 119-121, 130, 132-134, 153, 165-166,

big questions 20-21

Blake, William 98

Boyd, Gregory 148

Bracken, Joseph 62

Calvin, John 77

Campus Crusade for Christ 108-109

Center for Open and Relational Theology xi, 151

certainty 11, 14-15, 33-35, 43, 74, 139, 166

child abuse 16

chocolate ice cream 34-35

Christian denominations 149

Church 154

co-creating 91-93

conventional theology 14-20, 31, 37-39, 42, 44, 50-53, 64, 77-78,

81, 85-86, 88, 91, 93, 100, 104-105,
110, 118, 122-128, 132-133, 141-
143, 166
Covid-19 8-10, 136, 166
creatio ex nihilo 62, 94

Dante 3
deconstruction 132, 144, 154
Dellio, Ilia 95
Depeche Mode 130

ecology 154
ecology / caring for
creation 96-97
Evangelicalism 108, 142, 150,
evangelism 127
evolution 69, 74, 94-95
experiential / experience 101-102

faith 127-130
fate 35
feminism 22, 150, 155
Ford, Lewis 62
free / freedom / free will 7-8, 10,
20-24, 33-35, 44-45, 68-75, 79-
80, 85, 138-139, 155

God Can't 85-87
God / Deity
Abba 83
amipotence 81-82, 87-88,
113, 140
angry 18
authoritative 11-12, 19, 165

benevolent 11-12, 19, 122, 134, 165
changes / mutable 37-41, 44,
51, 58, 103
companion / friend 45, 53-55,
60-61, 131-132
controlling boyfriend 19-20, 24
creator 91-95
critical 11, 13, 19, 165
dipolar / essence-experience
binate 39-41, 166
distant 11-13, 78, 185
emotions 13, 20, 31, 52-53, 56,
57-58, 99-100, 155
everlasting relations 63-64
fellow-sufferer 68
foreknowledge 17, 33-35, 43, 84,
125, 136, 138, 155, 166, 169
germaphobe 17
giving and receiving 31, 62, 64,
122, 128
ground of being 80, 131
healer 68
holy 17, 103, 108
immaterial 58
impassable / unaffected /
uninfluenced 13, 16, 50-52
impersonal 130-133
in a box 55-56
in control, controlling 16-20, 24,
43-44, 73, 77, 78-80, 81, 85-
87, 124, 36-137, 140, 156
incorporeal / bodiless 55
intervening 17-19, 78
jerk 19-20

knowledge 4-6, 16-17, 30, 33-37, 41-44, 52-53, 84, 88, 95, 100, 123, 136, 138-139, 155, 166, 169

learns 36-38

loving 3-5, 10-11, 16, 19-23, 30, 40, 42, 50-51, 56, 64, 75, 79, 82-85, 96, 103, 112-113, 117, 119, 124-126, 128, 132-133, 136-137, 140-144

narcissist 17, 121-122

omnipresent 50, 55, 83-84, 88, 100-102, 108

parent 82-84

perceiving 99-100

perfect being 23

personal 56-57

power 81-88

relentless love 112-113

repents 31

schizophrenic 19

sovereignty / omnipotent 6-7, 11, 20, 24, 56, 77, 81-82, 113

steadfast / reliable 37-40

suffering / empathy 52-53

timelessness 24, 30-32, 41-42, 63-64, 116

trinity 61-64

unintelligible 19

hell 3-4, 17, 21, 104-106, 108, 112-113

Henry, Carl 38

heresy x, 53, 63

Hitler, Adolf 4

Holy Spirit 98, 156

hope 110-113

Houston Astros 33

image of God 53-55

immortality 110-113

intuition x, 15, 21-22, 44-45, 105, 123, 124, 129, 132, 134

Islam / Muslim 21, 52, 142, 150

jazz 27-28

Jesse Owens 14

Jesus 2, 23, 62, 83, 100, 104, 108, 119-120, 124, 127-130, 133-135, 139, 142, 159

John the Apostle 128

Judaism / Jew 6, 21, 30, 51, 62, 150, 156

Keller, Catherine 148

Largent, Steve 101

LGBTQ 6-7, 142

logic of love 21, 78-79

love, advantages 122-125

love, for God 133-135

love, framework 117-118

love, meaning of 133-134

love, open and relational theology 117-144

Luther, Martin 126

Maimonides 51

mansplaining 20

meaning / purpose 7, 24, 108, 118, 131, 138-139, 143-144

mental disability 9

Molinism / middle knowledge 166

Moltmann, Jürgen 62

movie analogy 32

Muir, John 143

mystery 8, 19, 78-79, 84, 136

Napoleon 29

natural laws 13, 17, 28

Nazi Holocaust 16

Northwind Theological Seminary 151, 161

Nygren, Anders 119-122

Oord, Thomas Jay 151

open and relational theology reasons 20-24

open future 22, 33-34, 43-44, 147

open theology 147-149, 157

Owyhees 126

pandemic 8-9

panentheism 100-130, 157

pantheism 103

parenting 12-13, 72, 82-83

Paul the Apostle 127-130, 140

perfect friend 60-61

perfection 23-24, 37-38

pet rocks 131-133

photography 98-99

Polkinghorne, John 95

possibilities 29, 33, 36, 45, 88, 93

Powers, Greg 131

prayer 4-6, 16, 30, 41-44, 52-53, 87, 131, 139-140, 158

predestine / predetermine / predecide / foreordain 8, 16, 21, 23, 27, 32, 33-34, 42, 73, 77, 106, 110, 118, 124, 125, 136, 138

problem of evil 84-87

process theology 147-148, 158

punk band 29

purgatory 13, 112

Qur'an 11, 21, 31

rape / sexual abuse x, 1-2, 20, 33, 60, 77, 84, 135-136

receiving love 58-60

relational theology 147-149, 159

religious pluralism 87, 142, 159-150, 159

Rwandan Genocide 30

Saint Patrick's Bad Analogies 63

salvation 105-110

San Jose 6

sanctification / turning points 109-110

Santa Claus 13

Sawtooth Mountains 3

science 23, 68, 69-72, 95-96, 117, 128-129, 132, 141, 154

science and religion 20, 23, 95, 151

self-love 125-126

separation from God 108-109

sexual reproduction 92

sin 17, 103, 108-109, 131

soccer 40

social justice 143

social sciences 22

Sproul, R.C. 141

string analogy 49-50

suffering x, 8-9, 23, 31, 52-53, 57, 85-86, 113, 118, 123, 129-130, 136-138, 142

survey of theology 10-13

theopoetics 99, 150, 153

Thomas Aquinas 50-51

time 27-32, 41-44, 55, 62-63, 160

torture x, 3, 20, 33, 54, 79, 84

Tuggy, Dale 62

unanswered prayer 33-34

uncontrolling love 80, 85, 124, 126

Unitarianism 62

Walla Walla, Washington 58-59

Ward, Keith 62

Whitehead, Alfred North 98-99

Zorn, Jim 101

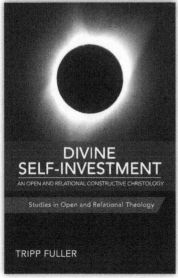
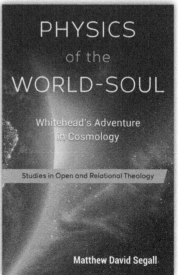

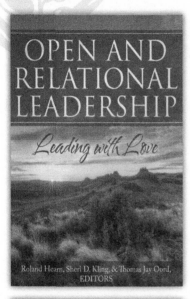
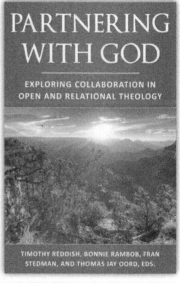
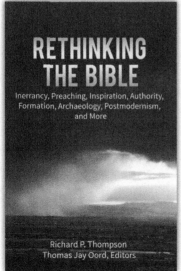
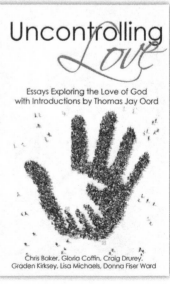

91107075R00114